# CONVICTION

# OXFORD SOCIO-LEGAL STUDIES

*General Editors*: J. Maxwell Atkinson, Donald R. Harris, R. M. Hartwell

Oxford Socio-Legal Studies is a series of books and conference proceedings published by the Centre for Socio-Legal Studies, Wolfson College, Oxford (a research unit of the Social Science Research Council). The series is concerned generally with the relationship between law and society, and is designed to reflect the increasing interest in this field of lawyers, social scientists and historians.

*Published titles*

J. Maxwell Atkinson and Paul Drew: ORDER IN COURT: The Organisation of Verbal Interaction in Judicial Settings

Ross Cranston: REGULATING BUSINESS: Law and Consumer Agencies

David P. Farrington, Keith Hawkins and Sally M. Lloyd-Bostock (editors): PSYCHOLOGY, LAW AND LEGAL PROCESSES

Sally M. A. Lloyd-Bostock: PSYCHOLOGY IN LEGAL CONTEXTS: Applications and Limitations

Mavis Maclean and Hazel Genn: METHODOLOGICAL ISSUES IN SOCIAL SURVEYS

Doreen J. McBarnet: CONVICTION: Law, the State and the Construction of Justice

*Forthcoming titles*

Alan Paterson: THE LAW LORDS

Donald R. Harris, Mavis Maclean and Hazel Genn: COMPENSATION AND SUPPORT FOR ILLNESS AND INJURY

Keith Hawkins: ENVIRONMENT AND ENFORCEMENT: the Social Construction of Pollution

Genevra Richardson, Anthony Ogus and Paul Burrows: POLICING POLLUTION: A Study of Regulation and Enforcement

Philip Lewis and Robert Dingwall (editors): LAW AND THE SOCIOLOGY OF THE PROFESSIONS

Paul Fenn and Yvonne Brittan: THE ECONOMICS OF ILLNESS AND INJURY

Berny Rubin and David Sugarman (editors): LAW, ECONOMY AND SOCIETY, 1700–1918

# CONVICTION
## Law, the State and the
## Construction of Justice

Doreen J. McBarnet
*SSRC Centre for Socio-Legal Studies,*
*Wolfson College, Oxford*

*First published 1981 by*
THE MACMILLAN PRESS LTD
*London and Basingstoke
Companies and representatives
throughout the world*

ISBN 0-333-25536-4

*Printed in Hong Kong*

# Contents

# Acknowledgements

I should like to thank all the people who have helped in this research: all those involved in the cases observed; the defendants, witnesses, lawyers and court personnel who talked to me or provided access to information; the colleagues who have offered comments and criticisms at various stages, including Chris Whelan, Keith Hawkins and Max Atkinson, Sir Rupert Cross and particularly Andrew Ashworth, Don Harris and Bert Moorhouse who took the trouble to read and comment on the whole final manuscript; and the secretaries who patiently transformed illegible scribbles into neat typescript, especially Chris Storrar and Noel Harris. Sections of chapters 3, 4 and 5 have been developed from articles originally published in P. Carlen (ed.), *Sociology of Law*, Sociological Review Monograph, Keele, 1976, and G. Littlejohn *et al.*, *Power and the State*, British Sociological Association, Croom Helm, 1978. Thanks are due to the publishers for permission to include revised and developed versions in this book.

Doreen J. McBarnet
December 1979

# 1 Introduction

This book began as a study of the routine operation of the criminal courts but has become a study of how the state rules through law. It was inevitably led in this direction by taking an approach unusual for a sociological study, focusing not so much on the routine interaction of the people who enforce the law but on the structure, substance and procedure of the law itself. Law is significant not just as the book of rules for criminal justice; it is also the means by which the democratic state rules. Law, then, provides a bridge between the traditional micro-theoretical concerns of criminal justice and the macro-theoretical issues of the state and dominant ideology. This book is thus about the construction of justice not simply at the level of how verdicts are routinely accomplished but at the more fundamental level of how one central aspect of the ideology of the democratic state works.

## LAW AND THE PROCESS OF CONVICTION[1]

Behind the verdict of the criminal court lies a process of conviction—conviction in two senses; first how judges[2] or juries come to *be convinced* beyond reasonable doubt of the appropriate verdict; second how that verdict so routinely, according to the statistics, comes to be a verdict of guilt. The verdict is the product of a process of conviction in both the subjective and the legal senses.

The conviction process in the legal sense poses a problem for explanation because it raises a strange paradox. All the rhetoric of justice we are so familiar with presents a picture of a system of criminal justice bending over backwards to favour the defendant rather than the prosecution. Every accused has the right to a fair trial. He is innocent till proved guilty; it is the prosecutor who must prove his case. What is more, the accused has a right to silence, he is not a compellable witness and he need not incriminate himself, so that the prosecutor has to be able to prove his case without the co-operation of the accused. The police for their part cannot arrest or search on suspicion to *find* evidence but only in relation to an already specified offence. They cannot force anyone to answer questions and must give a caution before asking them. Evidence for the prosecution case cannot therefore be collected or presented by *any* means but only within the limits set by law to safeguard the citizen. The accused *need* prove nothing, but can choose if he wishes to establish a defence case to counter that of the prosecution with the less stringent requirement not of 'proof' but merely of raising a reasonable doubt, and he may use legal expertise to do that. The whole flavour of the rhetoric of justice is summed up in the idea that it is better for ten guilty men to go free than for one innocent man to be wrongly convicted. Why then the paradox that the vast majority of cases processed through a criminal justice system so geared to favouring the accused results in a finding of guilt?

For they do. According to the criminal statistics for 1978, conviction rates were as follows: 90 per cent of Scottish cases involving crimes, 95 per cent of Scottish cases involving offences, 84 per cent of English Crown Court cases, 93 per cent of indictable cases, 95 per cent of non-indictable cases, in the English magistrates' courts.[3] Some samples show even higher rates—a 98.5 per cent conviction rate for magistrates' courts in Sheffield (Bottoms and McClean, 1976). Conviction depends in court on the plea or the verdict. If the accused pleads guilty to the charge against him, conviction follows as a matter of routine. If he pleads not guilty, a contested trial follows. According to Bottoms and McClean, 72.5 per cent of those contesting the case in magistrates' courts, 55 per cent of those choosing jury trials, and 71 per cent of those allocated to the higher courts were convicted on some or all counts (pp. 106, 209). In the rhetoric of justice everyone is entitled to a fair trial; yet most defendants plead guilty. In the rhetoric of justice any reasonable doubt should result in acquittal; yet for the clear majority of cases the court is convinced *beyond* reasonable doubt, despite all the rhetorical hamstrings on police and prosecution, that the accused is guilty. Why?

One answer might be quite simply that the defendants *are* guilty; the case against them is too strong to be plausibly disputed; the facts speak for themselves. Sir Robert Mark has suggested indeed that the very limitations placed on police and prosecution bringing a case to court make it highly probable that only the indisputably guilty come through the process at all:

The procedural safeguards for the suspect or accused in our system of criminal justice are such that committal for trial, involving the participation of lawyers and bench, is itself an indication of strong probability of guilt. (Alderson, 1973, p. 16)

But this is where we come to the process of conviction in its other, subjective, sense. Given the ambiguities and uncertainties that dog real-life incidents, how are clear-cut facts of the case and strong cases produced? How do judges and juries come to be persuaded *beyond reasonable doubt* by one case or another? Evidence, the facts of the case, strong and weak cases are not simply self-evident absolutes; they are the end-product of a process which organises and selects the available 'facts' and constructs cases for and in the courtroom. Behind the facts of the case that convince judges or juries to an unambiguous verdict lies a process of construction and a structure of proof that need to be probed and analysed.

Mark's point raises another question. What exactly *are* the procedures of criminal justice that are so readily assumed to protect the accused? For though they are constantly referred to in theory and in practice they are remarkably little investigated.

Sociologists have taken the question of how the criminal justice process works in relation to the principles of law by investigating only one side of the equation, the operation of justice, not the law itself. Explicitly or implicitly the question underlying sociological analysis of the criminal justice process always seems to be concerned with why the people who routinely operate the law also routinely depart from the principles of justice—depart from them in either or both of two ways—violating the principle of equality before the law by being more likely to arrest, convict, or sentence with greater severity lower- rather than middle- or upper-class people, blacks rather than whites, men rather than women; violating the principle of a criminal justice system geared to safeguarding the accused by routinely subverting the rights surrounding arrest, the right to a trial, the right to be presumed innocent till proved guilty.

So we are presented with a picture of how social and human factors undermine the workings of a criminal justice system geared to constraining state officials and favouring the accused. One study after another shows up class, race, and sex prejudices on the part of magistrates and policemen; bureaucratic pressures pushing the police into acceptable arrest rates, lawyers into negotiating pleas, court officials into a speedy rather than necessarily a just throughput of cases; personal ambitions, friendships, enmities, pressures from family and colleagues affecting the way justice is administered. The fact that courts and police stations are not just legal institutions but the daily work-places of policemen, lawyers, clerks of court, leads to the development of stereotypes, networks of shared understandings, alliances of alleged adversaries, techniques for routinising the work of policing or processing cases, to a situation where the suspect or defendant is the only one who is not part of the routine, is mystified by the language, bureaucracy, and processes of justice. Interaction on the beat, information games, remedial routines, degradation ceremonies in court, all help explain in fascinating and colourful detail why criminal justice operates as it does.[4]

What is barely touched on is the nature and role of the law itself. In a way it is not surprising. Law, like so many of our significant institutions, does not invite study. The statutes written in the dullest and most convoluted of prose, the shelves and shelves of dusty law reports, and the maze of common law decisions they contain can hardly raise the same immediate interest as the fascination of observing people in action, policemen ferrying drunks home from carnivals, lawyers negotiating and string-pulling, clerks of court organising cases round the tea break. But the failure to investigate the law is based on more theoretical grounds too, on an aversion to the naive role theory which equated formal rules and roles on how people *should* behave with how they *do*, which confused the prescriptive with the descriptive and presented people as passive puppets. Interactionist studies focused instead on the active nature of human beings, on the interactive processes by which the working of any institution was accomplished, on the personal and social variables which intervene between how institutions should work and how they do. In the realm of criminal justice the formal structures and rules of law were quite simply not a relevant subject for investigation.

Ironically, however, some vague notion of 'the law' is usually there as a background assumption, as a vague standard from which the law-enforcers under study are assumed to deviate. The same polarities appear again and again. The criminal justice system is seen in Packer's (1964) terms as modelled on 'due process' with law-enforcement agencies making it veer in practice towards 'crime control'; the 'law in the books' is presented as subverted by the 'law in action'. The assumption has been in effect that the law incorporates rights for the accused, and the problem has been simply to ask why and how the police and courts subvert, negate or abuse them. Thus Skolnick (1966) notes that the purpose of his book is 'not to reveal that the police violate rules and regulations—that much is assumed' (p. 22). In conventional sociological studies of criminal justice then, 'law' stands merely as a supposed standard from which the enforcers of law routinely deviate; legal procedures are simply *assumed* to incorporate civil rights. The 'law in action' is scrutinised but what the 'law in the books' actually says is simply taken as read; it remains unproblematic and unexplored.

At the level of policy rather than explanation the same assumption is made. Throughout the debate of the 1970s both those advocating law geared more to crime control, like Sir Robert Mark, or his successor as Metropolitan Police Commissioner, Sir David McNee, *and* those advocating more effective civil rights, like the National Council for Civil Liberties, tend to assume that the law does incorporate safeguards for the accused. Hence from one perspective the police are too hamstrung by the law to do their job and the guilty go free; from the other, the law does not work because the police abuse it to secure convictions. So NCCL writers note:

> All policemen are under the same pressure; *bend the rules* to deliver the goods in the form of convictions. . . . It is the *abuse* of police powers in these circumstances—arrest, search and questioning—that has created the most intractable police/civil liberty problem in recent years. (Cox, 1975, p. 164; my emphasis)

Likewise the Criminal Law Revision Committee's proposals to modify the right to silence were based on the assumption that current law does incorporate some such right, while its critics assume the same. So the liberal lawyers group, Release (1973), could say:

> At present, the only protection offered by the law to a man facing accusations from the police or other officials is his right to remain silent. If, as so often happens, a man is arrested late at night, taken to a police station and interrogated by several police officers using the methods that we have already described, he has the right to say: 'I wish to remain silent, I will not be questioned. I will not be intimidated or bullied. I will not incriminate myself, my friends, or my family as you wish me to do.' He is entitled to

say this without running the risk of anyone at a later stage being able to argue that by refusing to speak when questioned, he showed himself to be guilty of the accusation against him.

It is the intention of the CLRC to remove this sole protection. According to their proposals, failure to mention any fact later relied on in his defence, would expose the defendant to 'adverse inferences' in court. In other words, the jury or magistrates would be entitled to regard silence as evidence of guilt. (p. 26)

Champions, critics, and students of the criminal process alike, then, base their arguments on *assumptions* about the law. But does the law incorporate due process, safeguards for the accused, civil rights? The vague notion of 'due process' or 'the law in the books' in fact collapses two quite distinct aspects of law into one: the general principles around which the law is discussed—the rhetoric of justice—and the actual procedures and rules by which justice or legality are operationalised. The rhetoric used when justice is discussed resounds with high-sounding principles but does *the law* incorporate the rhetoric? This cannot simply be assumed; the law itself, not just the people who operate it, must be put under the microscope for analysis.

This is the approach which this study adopts. It focuses not on the interaction of policeman and citizen, lawyer and client, magistrate and defendant *per se* but on the legal context in which that interaction takes place. It supplements the interactionist approach by asking a different question. Instead of showing why police, magistrates, and lawyers might be motivated or pressurised into processing people as they do, it asks why they *may* process people as they do. That involves looking not at the informal rules of social interaction but at the formal rules of the law itself, at what is permitted or prohibited by statute, at what judges treat as acceptable, accountable, or sanctionable police and court practices.

In short, this study approaches the paradox of a high conviction rate in a legal system allegedly geared in favour of the accused by scrutinising the legal system itself. It turns 'the law' from a background assumption of interactionist research into a central sociological problem in itself. It does so for three reasons. The first is quite simply a need for information. Both theoretical and policy debate in the area of criminal justice are based on an assumption about the law which may be false. The second is the potential influence of the law on its enforcers. Interactionist scepticism regarding those who equate the prescriptive with the descriptive is entirely valid, but to say people do not *necessarily* obey the rules is not to say they never do. The law *can* constrain, especially when it is public and subject to controls. The law itself is also one of the contextual elements of decisions. Bureaucracy, colleagues, and personal ambitions do not have a monopoly on shaping decisions. The law itself may incorporate pressures and inducements which motivate decisions by policemen, lawyers, and defendants. What is more the rules may be facilitative as well as prohibitive. Law is, for example, one of the raw materials that lawyers work with. This book is full of illustrations of how lawyers use the law in courts to score points for their own case or against their adversary's. Clearly they act upon that raw material; they use it; but they are able to use it because it is there, able to use it *openly* because it is legitimate, because they *may* make their case in that way according to the law. The role of formal law in how the process of conviction is achieved should not be underplayed.

The third reason shifts the theoretical ground completely. Interactionist studies of criminal justice have scorned the study of formal rules because they were more concerned with what law-enforcers *do* than with what they *should* do: what they *should* do is, however, from a quite different theoretical perspective, a legitimate question to ask. It raises issues not so much about the operation, as about the politics of criminal justice.

## LAW, THE STATE AND DOMINANT IDEOLOGY

Studies of law-enforcement so far have in fact been less about the law than about occupational groups who happen to operate the law and incidentally impinge on it, a significant issue but not the only one. Law-enforcement analysed instead from the perspective of how it is meant to operate provides a more direct entrée into the nature of the law itself and the judicial and political élites of the state who make it. Here methods scorned for studying how the police and courts operate become vital for studying the law. Law reports may not tell us much about the actuality of police and courtroom behaviour but they do tell us what kind of behaviour is acceptable in law. Analysis of the 'law in the books' does not tell us what police and court officials do but a good deal about what they are legally allowed and legally expected to do. Law-enforcement, in short, is not exclusively an area for interactionist study at the micro level; it is also an issue in the politics of law at the macro level. This means a change of focus, shifting attention from the routine activities of petty officials of the state to the top of the judicial and political hierarchies where rules are made and sanctions operated, switching our question from the effectiveness or otherwise of rules and sanctions (assuming they were intended to be effective) to the intentions themselves. The question of whether the law does incorporate civil rights as in the ideology of legality it should, thus takes on a new significance. It is not just relevant to the structural framework within which petty officials routinely operate, it is also relevant to the *action*, the *intentions* of those at the top of the legal hierarchy. In that sense the micro-sociological conception of people and analysis of action is simply moved up the power structure, from those who administer the law to those who make it. But at the same time macro-sociological issues are raised too. Shifting the focus to the political and judicial élites also shifts the focus to the very core of the operation of the state.

To question whether the law incorporates its own rhetoric is to ask whether deviation from standards of justice and legality are not merely the product of informalities and unintended consequences at the level of petty officials, but institutionalised in the formal law of the state. This has implications for how the state rules. One of the essential justifications of the democratic state is precisely that it is based on legality, that the relationship between the state and the individuals of civil society is one governed not by the arbitrary exercise of power but by power exercised within the constraints of law. The criminal justice process is the most explicit coercive apparatus of the state and the idea that police and courts can interfere with the liberties of citizens only under known law and by means of *due process* of law is thus a crucial element in the ideology of the democratic state. To question whether the law in fact incorporates the rhetoric of justice is to question the ideological foundations of the state. It is to raise the possibility of contradictions within dominant ideology and questions about the mechanics of its management. It is to raise questions about what the whole idea of the rule of law means and how it operates.

It is a long way from the Saturday night affray to the Law Lords; a world of meaning separates the breach of the peace or burglary or assault and theories of how the state rules. Yet they are inextricably interlinked. This study tries to take one small step to bridge the gap.

## METHODS AND DATA

This research began as an observational study in the courts; 105 cases (referred to throughout the book by case numbers 1 to 105) were observed in the sheriff and district courts of Glasgow, under the jurisdictions of stipendiary and lay magistrates, sheriffs sitting alone, and sheriffs sitting with a jury. The nature of the study led to textbooks on the rules of evidence and procedure, mainly at that stage as background information. They in turn led to law reports and statutes in a naive attempt to pin down what exactly the law was, and the law of criminal procedure and evidence itself, first its substance, then its very form, became a central focus of analysis. The study therefore draws on both observed empirical data, along with some informal interviews with lawyers, policemen, defendants and witnesses, and an analysis of law reports, statutes, committee reports, and legal texts.

The empirical data are mainly Scottish; the study of law ranges over both Scots and English law. In evidence, procedure, the structure of trial and prosecution they vary far less than is sometimes supposed, and where they vary the impact is not always significant. This is not, however, a comparative study. It simply shows how both Scots and English law define and affect the conviction process; where there are marked differences they are noted and where a point specific to English law requires empirical illustration it is done by drawing on observation in English courts conducted in the course of a more recent project.[5]

Taking the approach of examining law and the legal system itself has meant taking on board data more normally associated with 'lawyers' law' than with sociology. There are risks in doing this, risks of being accused by sociologists of being unsociological, by purists of being eclectic, risks particularly of criticism by lawyers. The sociologist is an amateur in the field of law and risks quite simply getting it wrong. Yet the law is not such a mystical area; it takes time but it is accessible. Indeed as evidence of the discourse of the powerful it provides via the law reports a veritable bank of readily available data. Sociologists may, in pointing out how defendants are mystified by the law, also have been too readily deterred by the mystique themselves. The risks are not merely worth taking; they are necessary steps if the sociology of law is to move beyond being the sociology of just another set of occupational groups and become truly a sociology of *law*.

## THE STRUCTURE OF THE BOOK

Chapter 2 begins in very general terms by setting the process of conviction in the context of the structure and meaning of legal proof. Chapters 3 to 6 examine in detail the statutory rules and case law rulings which provide the legal context for the guilty plea, define the methods that can be legitimately used by police, lawyers, and judges, and set out the legal powers, privileges, and prohibitions involved in the production, preparation, and presentation of evidence for trial. They show how it is *legally* possible for the prosecution case to win so routinely *despite* the rhetoric of a criminal justice system bending over backwards to constrain the prosecution and safeguard the accused. Chapter 7 examines the structure of the courts, the division into first- and second-class tiers, and the ideology of summary justice. Throughout the book there are suggestions as to how the gap between law and rhetoric is managed, how the rhetoric of justice survives its routine denial in law. Chapter 8 addresses this question more explicitly and draws out the implications for the whole idea of the rule of law in the democratic state.

# 2 Convincing the court: The Structure of Legal Proof

The core of the liberal democratic concept of criminal justice is that a person is innocent *until proved guilty*. Justice does not rule out punishment; on the contrary it deals in 'just deserts'. What the ideology of justice is opposed to is *arbitrary* punishment. The important criterion in dealing out 'just deserts' is that the recipient should have been *proved* guilty. The whim of kings, the barbarism of joust, the mysticism of magic should be replaced by a rational method of proof. The trial is where that process of proof is not only carried out but put on public display—where justice has not only to be done, but be seen to be done. The plausibility of the trial as a process of *proving* the accused guilty is one criterion by which the ideology of justice stands or falls.

But the trial is not self-evidently a process of proof. 'What happened', the incident under investigation or in dispute cannot be conceived of as some absolute—'truth' or 'reality'—nor as a simple objective thing, a jigsaw puzzle that can be taken to pieces and reassembled through witnesses' testimony exactly as it happened. First, the limits are not so clearly defined, for how is reality bounded? Where of all the events going on continuously and simultaneously in several lives did 'the incident' start and stop? Second, the pieces do not fit so neatly together. Conceptions of reality vary. 'What happened' is, to a witness, what *struck* him as happening; how he made sense of what he saw. Different witnesses with different perceptive filters may be struck in different ways. Truth and reality are subjective and relative. Third, the pieces are dynamic: 'what happened' is, to a witness, not just how he made sense of it at the time but how he has made sense of it reconstructing it later; not just how well but *how* he remembers it. And of course there are lies: witnesses may have vested interests more powerful than the oath. The *idea* of proving what happened is a complicated philosophical problem.

Not that the law admits to this. Witnesses are simply enjoined to 'tell the truth, the whole truth and nothing but the truth', a fine piece of rhetoric, devastatingly naive and blasé, but also extremely powerful. In what must be the most familiar of all courtroom catchphrases it deftly sweeps all the philosophical problems neatly under the carpet of mystique. But analytically the problems remain. Indeed when one adds the fact that most trials take place months if not years after the incident in question, and that the court in an adversary system is presented with two conflicting versions of that incident, it becomes incredible that any jury or magistrate can ever feel that what happened has been proved beyond question. Yet in the vast majority of trials it seems they are. The philosophical problem of how one reproduces 'reality' thus becomes a sociological one: how is it that in such a situation of ambiguity, conflict, subjectivity, fading or moulded memories, the judges of the facts can so readily find themselves convinced beyond reasonable doubt?

In part the answer lies in the skills of advocacy, 'the technique of persuasion', as David Napley (1975) puts it, but these skills are themselves merely adaptations to a particular structure of proof. This chapter focuses on the legal *concept* of proof and the legal *form* of proof as they have developed in the common law countries since the seventeenth century.


## THE CONCEPT OF PROOF

The legal system copes with the philosophical problems of proof by redefining it into more manageable proportions. What is involved is not a philosophical or scientific concept of proof but a much less demanding *legal* concept. As David Napley (1975) puts it in teaching the techniques of the advocate:

> Whilst therefore the doctor and the scientist are engaged in an inquisitional pursuit in which they are seeking the truth, the lawyer is engaged in an accusatorial pursuit to see whether a limited area of proof has been discharged. (p. 30)

The justification lies not in any idealism that 'the truth the whole truth and nothing but the truth' results, but in pragmatics. The courts are there not to indulge in the impossible absolutes of philosophy or science but to reach decisions—quickly:

> If we lived for a thousand years instead of about sixty or seventy, and every case was of sufficient importance, it might be possible, and perhaps proper . . . to raise every possible enquiry as to the truth of statements made. . . . In fact mankind finds it impossible. (Rolfe, in *A.-G.* v. *Hildicock*, 1847, cited in Cross, 1974, p. 21)

So the courts have drawn a line at what will do as proof. Prosecutors do not have to prove everything a jury might want to know, they only have to produce a *sufficiency* of evidence. Juries have to be convinced beyond reasonable doubt—but they cannot choose the issues that they have to be convinced about: sufficiency and credibility are distinguished in law. The law defines how much evidence constitutes 'sufficient' to prove a case and it is the judge's role to decide that this standard has been met. The jury's role is to decide whether they believe it. But the legal demands involved in 'sufficiency' are often rather lower than one might expect. Indeed from judges' summing-up addresses it seems clear they recognise they have to persuade juries—whose only knowledge of the law is after all the rhetoric—that *enough* evidence is not as much as they might think.

In Case 103 where the accused was charged with theft but the goods were still alongside the car they had been stolen from, the judge took pains to point out this was not mere attempt but legally constituted theft:

> But note this, ladies and gentlemen, [then he picked up and read from a legal text] it is sufficient to complete the crime of theft if the thing be removed for the shortest time and [loudly] *but a small distance* . . .

and he continued for two minutes with the details.

In Case 91 the judge addressed the jury:

> You might expect you would need an eye-witness for proof, but that is not necessary in cases of theft. There are facts and circumstances from which theft can be inferred without eye witnesses. Here the Crown can infer theft according to the doctrine of recent possession . . .

In Case 93, where one of the charges was breach of the peace, the judge (the same one as in Case 103) again read from a law book on the definition of the offence (having prefaced the law with the comment that this was a common but fundamental offence, 'because without the peace there is no order, and if there is no order there is certainly no civilisation as we have been brought up to know it'):

> Breach of the peace is behaviour which "might reasonably be expected to lead to lieges being upset". Note that "might be". There is no need to lead evidence that anyone *was* upset.

He continued on the question of evidence for the second charge of assault with an ornamental sword:

> It was perhaps revealing that the accused's idea of assault was an idea held by many—hitting a person. That is not the law. An assault in law [and out comes the book again] is an intentional attack on the person of another whether it injures him or not. To aim a blow at a victim is an assault though the blow never lands, to set a dog on someone, to make a gesture of violence are all assaults. Disabuse yourself of the idea that there's got to be blood, got to be bruises. To aim a blow, a fist, a boot [pause] a *sword*, [pause] is assault.

Likewise a Scottish jury will be told that there must be corroboration for proof of a case, but they are not left with that as a *minimum* requirement to work from; they are not left to decide whether the general idea that two supporting pieces of evidence constitutes proof is valid; they are told it is. Corroboration equals legal sufficiency. The only question for the jury is whether they believe those two items of evidence, whether they are convinced by the evidence, *not* whether they are convinced by the assumption that such evidence constitutes proof.

They do still have to be convinced of the credibility of the evidence, of course; convinced indeed beyond reasonable doubt. They need not *all* be convinced though. The majority verdict institutionalises ignoring the doubts of two jurors in the 10:2 majority verdict allowed in England, seven in the 8:7 straight majority allowed in Scotland. Nor indeed do all doubts the juror may have count *per se* as 'reasonable doubts'. English judges have now been advised it is safer not to try and define a reasonable doubt but Scottish juries are warned in the judges' summing up that they cannot fail to convict because of 'frivolous' doubts or because of the 'strained or fanciful acceptance of remote possibilities' (*Irving* v. *Ministry of Pensions*, 1945). In Case 91 the judge warned that 'beyond reasonable doubt' meant 'not a philosophical doubt but a reasonable doubt'. In Case 103 the jury was told that proof beyond reasonable doubt:

> does not mean proved to a mathematical nicety because if that was so no case would ever be proved. Nor either does it mean a capricious doubt. It means doubt based on substance, and reason on the evidence before you. [And the judge thumped the table in emphasis.] If *such a doubt as that* exists the accused is entitled to the benefit of it.

In Case 93, the same judge began by reeling off the same definition almost verbatim, with a little extemporising as he concluded:

> If that was so, no criminal charge would ever be proved and God help us all then. Some doubting Thomases will doubt everything, even the evidence of their own eyes. You cannot indulge in that. Doubt must be based on substance and reason on the evidence before you.

The concept of 'proof beyond reasonable doubt' is thus redefined from the awesome heights of abstraction into pragmatic minimal standards that can be all too readily attained. At the same time the problem of 'unbounded reality' is tackled by the notions of admissibility[1] and relevance.

Relevance, with the related concepts of 'material' issues or 'the facts of the case' sets limits on what may be introduced as evidence or indeed on what may be taken into account as evidence: 'Your experience of him is limited to what you heard in that box. . . . Try the case according to the evidence.' (Case 93.) It is also interlinked with the accusatorial style of a trial: indeed in general terms it is this that gives it its substance: ultimately what is relevant is the facts of the accusation. The prosecutor thus sets the general boundaries of relevance in his charge. This point is also implied in Archbold's (1979) dictat (reserved only for defence counsel) that:

> the defence should exercise a proper discretion not to prolong the

case unnecessarily. It is no part of his duty to embark on lengthy cross-examination on matters which are not really in issue. (s. 525)

And it is the judge's duty to stop such irrelevant evidence. So in Case 29, the boys accused of suspicious activities around cars, who claimed they were in fact being arrested for nothing in order to be questioned about a stolen television set, were interrupted:

Magistrate: I'm sorry—I'm not prepared to listen to information about a television.
Accused: But he said he didn't ask us about a TV set and he did.
Magistrate: It's irrelevant to the charge.

Information relevant to the incident but irrelevant to the prosecution's framing of the charge is thus edited out. More generally, how the concept of relevance transcends the problems of truth may be best illustrated by this example:

Witness: The truth is, going back—you want the truth, you'll get the truth . . .
Assessor: [interrupting] Just a minute.
Magistrate: We're only concerned with what happened on this occasion. (Case 97)

The concept of relevance thus allows artificial boundaries to be drawn around unbounded reality, and 'the whole truth' to be replaced by 'the facts of the case'.

Indeed it is not just the concept of relevancy that does this; it is also the basic form by which proof is accomplished—by adversary advocacy.


## THE FORM OF PROOF

Adversary advocacy helps solve the philosophical problem of reproducing reality quite simply by not even attempting it. Instead the search for truth is replaced by a contest between caricatures. Advocacy is not by definition about 'truth' or 'reality' or a quest for them, but about arguing a case. The concept of a case is such a fundamental part of Western legal thought that we may take it for granted, but it is a method of proof with a history of only two or three centuries, and one which provides a neat example of the abstraction which theorists of law under capitalism, like Pashukanis (1978), see as an essential element of the legal form. Just as the concept of the legal subject abstracts him from his real social being, so the case abstracts from the complexity of experience, and in doing so it helps solve both the practical and the ideological problems of proof.

An incident and a case made out about the incident are not the same thing. Conceptions of reality are multifaceted and un-bounded; cases are 'the facts' as abstracted from this broad amorphous raw material. The good advocate grasps at complex confused reality and constructs a simple clear-cut account of it. A case is thus very much an edited version. But it is not just edited into a minimal account—a microcosm of the incident—it is an account edited with vested interests in mind. Hence the lawyer's approach 'that, so far as possible, only that should be revealed which supports his case' (Napley, 1975, p. 29). Far from being 'the truth, the whole truth and nothing but the truth' a case is a biased construct, manipulating and editing the raw material of the witnesses' perceptions of an incident into not so much an exhaustively accurate version of what happened as one which is advantageous to one side. In relation to an incident, then, a case is partial in both senses—partisan and incomplete. The good advocate is not concerned with reproducing incidents but producing cases, not with truth but with persuasion. Lord Denning makes this quite clear:

the duty of counsel to his client in a civil case—or in defending an accused person—is to make every honest endeavour to succeed. He must not, of course, knowingly mislead the court, either on the facts or on the law, but short of that, he may put such matters in evidence or omit such others as in his discretion he thinks will be most to the advantage of his client. So also, when it comes to his speech, he must put every fair argument which appears to him to help his client towards winning the case. The reason is because he is not the judge of the credibility of the witnesses or of the validity of the arguments. He is only the advocate employed by the client to speak for him, and present his case, and he must do it to the best of his ability, without making himself the judge of its correctness, but only of its honesty. Cicero makes the observation that it is the duty of the judge to pursue the truth, but it is permitted to an advocate to urge what has only the semblance of it. (*Tombling* v. *Universal Bulb Co. Ltd*, 1951)

The Bar is an apprentice-based craft, and the lectures and manuals on the art of advocacy by its 'masters' illustrate the same role. Sir William Boulton's *Conduct and Etiquette at the Bar* indeed quotes Denning's view, above, to summarise the advocate's role (1975, p. 69). Sir Malcolm Hilbery's *Duty and Art in Advocacy* takes pride in the transformation advocacy can bring to what witnesses have to say:

> His may be bad material, his opponent's good. One side is wrong and each side has its counsel. But even bad material treated by a good craftsman will take form and with that may even be made attractive. (Hilbery, 1975 p. 29)

Lord Cross observes proudly to the Holdsworth Club:

> I have seldom felt more pleased with myself than when I persuaded three out of five law lords to come to a conclusion I was convinced was wrong. (Cross, 1973, p. 3)

Coddington, in *Advice on Advocacy in the Lower Courts*, takes the same line, somewhat less pithily:

> One must never tell a lie oneself. One must never tell the witness to lie. On must never put forward a defence which one has been told by one's witness is not true. One must never express one's personal opinion of the truth and justice of one's case or of the reliability of a witness, because one speaks as an advocate not as a private person. But on the other hand, one is entitled to accept what one does not personally believe, if a witness has said it on his own account. One is entitled to argue that the court should accept this, that or the other evidence, whether one does so or not in one's own heart. (Coddington, 1954, p. 2)

And like all good writers of manuals on advocacy he cites an apocryphal case—the case of the trilby hat—to show what he means:

> There is an old Northern Circuit story that a woman was found

strangled on Ilkley Moor, and beside her body was a trilby hat which a witness recognised as that of the accused though it had no special marks of identification. Defence counsel cross-examined: 'Is not this a perfectly ordinary type of hat? Are there not thousands of others like it? Is it not an ordinary size? Would it not fit thousands of heads?' To all these the witness had to answer 'Yes'. At the conclusion of the prosecution Counsel submitted to the judge that there was not sufficient identification for the case to go to the jury. The judge agreed and told the jury to acquit. The prisoner was discharged, and as he was leaving the dock he turned to the judge and said 'And now pray Lord, may I'av my at?' (*ibid.*, p. 2)

The Bar's fondness for supporting descriptions of advocacy with apocryphal stories is itself a nice demonstration of the advocate's concern with a good story rather than an accurate one, while the habit of using such apocryphal stories in lectures and handbooks on advocacy, even if primarily to keep students awake with a joke, nonetheless suggests a latent socialisation function into manipulation and persuasion rather than 'truth'.

Of course there are professional ethics involved, for example, not arguing for a client one knows to be guilty, but there are also ways of coping even with this (spelt out alongside the statement of the ethic) namely by never asking a client directly if he is guilty, avoiding the ethic by making sure one does *not* know, or if the client volunteers the information anyway, by refraining from arguing a positive case *for* him in court, while nonetheless arguing against the opposing case (Napley, 1975, p. 43).

It is worth noting in passing that there are no such rules on arguing prosecution cases, just one example of the suspicion of guilt attached to the accused by virtue of being accused. On the contrary the prosecution's role is elevated in the manuals (Napley, 1975, p. 74; Boulton, 1975, p. 74) to one of public service, not just in Scotland where he is literally a civil servant, but in England where he is usually a barrister who may act either for defence or prosecution. In his defence role he is a biased advocate, as a prosecutor, an impartial 'minister of justice'. This role would seem to exist largely in ideology. Archbold, in a manual more concerned in the main with procedural rules than broad rhetoric, notes this prescription but on the same page lists legal rules which suggest the expectation of rather a different role. For example, it is noted that the prosecutor has a duty to give to the defence the names of witnesses whom he does not intend to call but who do have material evidence to offer (Archbold, 1979, s. 433). The word 'material' is the key. It indicates that the prosecutor is assumed to present a case selected for conviction rather than one that sets out all of even what *he* sees as the *material* facts. Again, the prescription for how and to what end examination-in-chief should be conducted—'to adduce relevant and admissible evidence to *support the contention* of the party who calls the witness'—makes no exception for the prosecuting counsel (*ibid.*, s. 512).

At the level of practice there is no doubt that prosecutors do act out the normal advocate's role of arguing a one-sided case: the examples throughout this book are readily supported officially by the Fisher Report on the *Confait* case, in which three youths—two of whom were mentally subnormal—were convicted of murder on the basis of impossible confessions—impossible, because it was subsequently proved that Confait could not possibly have died as late as the confessions alleged. But ambiguities over the time of death were filtered out by the police and prosecution in constructing and presenting their case. Fisher (1977) notes of the prosecutor's courtroom examination of a pathologist on the crucial issue of the time of death:

> It might well be that, if Dr C. had been given sight of the other evidence and asked to reconsider his evidence in the light of it, and had been asked the relevant questions in a neutral way instead of being asked to suggest ways in which the period for the time of death could be extended after midnight, the course of the trial would have been different and an acquittal might have resulted. (Fisher, 1977, p. 223)

Or again:

> . . . far from trying to make the time of death more precise, those concerned with the investigation and prosecution . . . made every effort to keep it as vague as possible. The reason for this was that they were concerned to establish a case which rested wholly or mainly on confessions which could not be entirely true unless the time of death was outside the brackets given by [the experts]. (*Ibid.*, p. 20)

Indeed a closer look at the legal sources suggests it would be very hard to find a *legal* prescription for the prosecutor to behave as a 'minister of justice'. The *Puddick* case from which the phrase is quoted and the *Banks* case which cited it as law, were cases of rape and unlawful carnal knowledge. The prescription made in *Puddick* was very much in relation to the specific difficulties of knowing what happened in sexual cases, and explicitly related to them, not to the role of the prosecutor in general:

> Counsel for the prosecution *in such cases* are to regard themselves as ministers of justice, and not to struggle for a conviction . . . (1865, p. 499, my emphasis)

What is more, the *Banks* appeal which tried to establish this as law *even* in a sexual case, was dismissed (1916).

Nonetheless the notion of the prosecutor as a 'minister of justice' not only functions at the ideological level both in the rhetoric of the Bar as to their role, and in general to support the view of a system of justice bending over backwards to ensure the innocent are not convicted, but is also an idea that is put to good practical use by prosecutors in court to support the credibility of their cases as opposed to the biased nature of the defence's:

> Prosecutor: Ladies and gentlemen, my function is to elicit as much evidence as possible to put before you. My friend's is to defend his client's best interests. *I* act in the public interest. (Case 103)

The emphasis in advocacy on both sides on persuasion rather than 'facts' is reflected in and promoted by the structure of the profession, with its separation of solicitors and barristers—a separation which incidentally is emphasised in the pages and pages of Boulton's *Conduct and Etiquette at the Bar* (1975) devoted to the rules of barrister–solicitor relations, right down to the undesirability of a barrister being an honorary member of a local law society, or of purchasing tickets for a local law society dinner (though there would be 'no objection to accepting gratuitous invitations'). The roles of the two should be quite distinct. The barrister is not allowed to interview witnesses. His task is to take as given the facts assembled by the solicitor and to argue from them not about them: Boulton asserts: 'It is essential that he should be able to rely on the

responsibility of a solicitor as to the state of the facts put before him'
(p. 8). Hilbery (1975) notes that 'a Barrister is required by his
professional code to make use of the material which is contained in
his instruction, and nothing else' (p. 11) and he has an extreme story
to demonstrate this with Mr Justice Swift, in his days as a counsel
recognising an opposing witness in a case of fraud as an ex-solicitor
once convicted of forgery and embezzlement, but concluding 'Well,
I cannot make use of it. It seems a pity.'

This separation of processing from presentation encourages a
narrow persuasive role with emphasis on skill in the use of words and
manipulation of witnesses rather than in any concept of search for
'what really happened'. It also means the barrister has no direct
experience of the negotiation that may have lain behind the 'facts'
as he has them, the questioning behind statements for example. He
may therefore argue for 'the facts of the case', without any
subjective knowledge of how they have been processed, and avoid
the ethical limitations on wilfully misleading the court. Working
from a prepared case, with its ambiguities and ifs and buts filtered
out, he may also argue the more convincingly. The public
presentation of evidence may thus carry an aura of subjective
conviction that is not just produced by the art of the advocate but by
the structure of the profession. The conceptual distinction in
advocacy between incident and case is hardened in the practical
separation of its private preparation by one professional and its
public presentation by another.

A further feature of the form of presenting proof is that it is
interrogatory. Evidence is not presented directly by witnesses, but
indirectly in response to questions by counsel. The rules prohibit
leading questions but the very framing of a question, whether
leading or not, and the context in which it occurs, set parameters on
what can be an acceptable answer. The witness is a respondent, 'he
is there to answer questions, that is all' (Cockburn, 1952, p. 10), and
the person who asks the questions is structurally very much in a
position of control (Atkinson and Drew, 1979) and quick to
interrupt witnesses or warn them to confine themselves to the
essential facts they are being asked about, or indeed merely to
answer yes or no:

Prosecutor      [to victim] Did you know him [the defendant]
                previously?
Witness:        Yes we had a scuffle the night before.

| Prosecutor | [sharply] Mr Sweeney, the question was very simple. Please answer yes or no. Don't volunteer anything. Understand? (Case 98) |
|---|---|

The questions 'should be clear and unambiguous and as short as possible, each raising a single point' (Walker and Walker, 1975, p. 360) so particularising and abstracting the facts relevant for the case from the multiple possible facts of the incident. This style of presentation helps construct an idea of clear-cut proof, by filtering and controlling the information witnesses make available to the court, and so transforming what could emerge as an ambiguous welter of vying and uncertain perceptions into 'the facts of the case'.

Interrogation means not just filtering potential information but imposing order and meaning upon it by the sequence and context of questions asked—whatever meaning it may have had to the witness, control by questioning can impose the meaning of the questioner. The case thus takes on its own logic within the framework of the 'facts of the case', and any other issues mentioned, hinted at or unknown, lose any relevancy to the meaning of the case that they may have had to the meaning of the incident. What is more the order and logic of a controlled case is much more visible than that in the welter of social reality, and therefore, arguably the more persuasive in carrying its evidence along. Questions can be both selected and ordered to lead, as it were inexorably, to a given conclusion, to proof.

Hence the style of asking a series of questions to which the individual answers must be 'yes', then summing them up into the logical total to which they add up—*logical* viewed in the abstract, but with an implication which would not of itself either reflect the incident, or be accepted as accurate *in toto* by the witness. This occurs not just in apocryphal tales of trilby hats but routinely in court:

| Prosecutor: | Weren't you making as much noise as the others? |
|---|---|
| Accused: | No I was trying to quieten them down. |
| Prosecutor: | You were saying 'Ssh' in a whisper? |
| Accused: | No I was saying 'be quiet or you'll get into trouble'. |
| Prosecutor: | And they were making a lot of noise. |
| Accused: | Yes. |
| Prosecutor: | So you had to raise your voice so they'd hear you. |
| Accused: | Well maybe a wee bit. |

Prosecutor: So you were shouting and bawling.
Accused: No.
Prosecutor: You just said you were! (Case 19)

The right of the advocate not just to question but to sum up—a right denied to the witnesses themselves—allows still further editing, abstraction, and imputation of meaning to be imposed on what witnesses say.

Interrogatory, adversary advocacy has another function. It not only organises proof; it also helps legitimise the outcome. Doing the best one can with a client's case means taking it to extremes, one side taking the grey areas of 'reality' and turning them into 'black', the other turning them to 'white'. This is why cross-examination is often no more than bringing ambiguity back into an extreme case. Being an artifice, adversary advocacy makes for thoroughly artificial ways of discrediting people. A witness's credibility is attacked by bringing into cross-examination *what he would have liked to say in examination*, given a chance to do so:

Prosecutor: You didn't tell my friend [the defence agent] that.
Defendant: He didn't ask me.
Prosecutor: You're on trial—did you not think it was up to you to say that.
Defendant: I've been told not to say other things. If he had asked me I'd have said it. (Case 103)

Indeed for a witness to suggest there *is* common ground, some truth in the adversary's version, rather than grossly distinct black and white cases, is also to invite imputations on his credibility:

Prosecutor: [to defendant] So only those bits of evidence that go against you aren't true? (Case 26)

But more generally the presentation of cases as mutually exclusive extremes provides a potent legitimation for whichever version is accepted—the whiteness of one extreme is all the more readily displayed by the blackness of the other. Wiping out the grey area means very often that to believe one case is necessarily not to believe the other.

The method of proof by advocacy thus focuses on the case not the incident; on manipulation, persuasion, and caricature, not 'truth' and so sweeps the problems attendant on reproducing 'what happened' neatly under the carpet. Both in its concepts and its form the legal system copes with the problems of proof and truth by redefining them. And the problem of how the judges of the facts can so readily find themselves convinced beyond reasonable doubt that a case is proved, is explained, in part, by the legal meaning attached to their task and the method by which they are presented with the information on which they must decide.

But the question of conviction is not just how juries or magistrates are *convinced*; it is also how they are convinced of *guilt*, particularly since the rules of evidence, the concept of admissibility, and the legal structure in general are so routinely presented as biased in favour of the accused. It is one thing to say the concept of the case obviates the philosophical problems of proof and truth; it is another to show how the prosecutor manages to construct a case in the face of all sorts of general principles which set limits on the methods by which evidence against the accused can be acquired and indeed exclude all kinds of information unfavourable to him. In assembling and presenting a case for conviction the police and prosecutor must abide by the demands of legality: how then is it that, in the face of such obstacles, the prosecution case normally succeeds? That is the question addressed in the next five chapters.

# 3 Police Powers and the Production of Evidence

Incrimination is the first step in the process of conviction. Essentially it is a question of gathering and presenting information that pins enough evidence on an individual to charge him with an offence. One major complaint by police and prosecution—voiced for example by Sir David McNee, the Metropolitan Police Commissioner, and Sir Thomas Hetherington, Director of Public Prosecution, in their evidence to the Royal Commission on Criminal Procedure[1]—is that legal procedures surrounding arrest, search, and interrogation of a suspect limit their ability to conduct satisfactory criminal investigations and acquire incriminating information. Certainly a glance at the broad principles governing these areas of investigation would confirm the problems involved.

For example, how are the police supposed to acquire evidence against someone by questioning him? They can, according to the Judges' Rules (Home Office, 1964) ask questions of anyone, suspected or not, but what they cannot do is force him to stay and answer them since (according to the judgement in *Christie* v. *Leachinsky* 1947) they cannot detain anyone against his will without charging him or telling him of the specific offence involved. But since they cannot charge someone till they have reasonable evidence against him they are back to square one. What is more, once they do charge someone, they may not then question him anyway (back to the Judges' Rules) while as soon as they have reasonable grounds to suspect him they should inform him of his right *not* to answer questions by cautioning him: 'You are not obliged to say anything unless you wish to do so but what you say may be put into writing and given in evidence.' (Home Office, 1964)

In principle then the police must have evidence against someone before detaining him, *not* detain him in order to obtain evidence against him—exactly the principle one might expect to be enunciated in an ideology of legality which seeks to safeguard the citizen from the state by prohibiting arbitrary arrest. At the level of abstract principle, due process and crime control seem well and truly at odds. And the question facing us is how do the police, in the face of legal definitions of due process, acquire the requisite information for incriminating suspects and setting the whole process in motion? The first step is to tease out a little more precisely what both crime and law mean in practice.

First, crime: how difficult the incrimination process is depends on the kind of offence involved. In what the police see as 'real police work' (Cain, 1971, p. 88) incrimination may well be problematic. For this is the stuff detective fiction is made of, where only the offence comes to light and both offender and evidence for incrimination have to be established by investigation. But this is not the kind of offence that dominates the work of either the police or the courts. Petty offences, particularly offences against public order, are much more typical and these are of quite a different nature. They are largely a matter of police–citizen encounter with the police defining marginal behaviour as subject to arrest or not, with the policeman and the culprit on the spot, with no investigation involved, and the process of incrimination simply begun and ended with the charge. In short for the vast majority of cases that are processed by the police and the courts, incrimination, and the constraints of law on incrimination, are simply *not* a problem. To that extent the police view must be put in perspective.

Of course the police demand for more powers is less concerned with such petty offenders than with the 'hardened criminals' who escape conviction by slipping through the net of procedures that are 'excessively solicitous towards accused persons'.[2] The irony is that the people most likely to be caught by wider police powers are the petty offenders who, as it were, know not what they do. Successful professional criminals are, as Mack (1976) notes and McIntosh (1971) demonstrates historically, successful professional criminals exactly because they can find their way round and adapt their methods to new procedure. To expect too much of a change in the rules is sociologically naive: too neat a cause–effect, mechanical model imposed on the negotiable and dynamic relationship between law and crime.

One consequence of the preoccupation in the police debate with 'hardened criminals' and 'real crime' is that lawyers have paid little attention to how the law affects minor offences, the vast majority though they are. Sociologists *have* studied the petty offences, indeed concentrated on them, but not in relation to the law. Their interest has been in the very marginality of the behaviour and thus with a different question: how and why the police come to define specific incidents and people as criminal. Hence the emphasis on the act of arrest, e.g. on interaction between police and black youths with the consequent arrest related to the policeman's perception of the youth's behaviour as lacking in sufficient deference (Sykes and Clark, 1975); on the selection for arrest via, e.g., police stereotyping of blacks, or lower-class people, or mods and rockers, or bohemians as likely law-breakers, trouble-makers, drug-takers (Skolnick, 1966; Young, 1971; Cohen, 1971); or on motivations behind the policeman's decision—personal ambitions, bureaucratic demands, the influence of family or colleagues (Cain, 1973)—to explain why the police make such arrests.

By concentrating on both the *topic* of these more marginal offences and the *question* of how police definitions are made, sociologists have quite logically been drawn into the operation of all sorts of *non-legal* influences on the police decision and away from the influence of the law itself. But the very fact that legal procedure was *not* a factor which they found confronting them much in their studies of routine police work is itself a matter worthy of some scrutiny. One simple, but significant point implied by Maureen Cain on why there are so many marginal arrests is that they are easy. What also requires investigation is why they are easy not just to carry out but to sustain in law.

## PROCESSING MARGINAL OFFENCES[3]

The rhetoric of legality prohibits arbitrary arrest, and in accord with this any arrest is accountable. But of course it is accountable only if it is challenged, and, as Renton and Brown (1972) point out in discussing arrest without warrant, 'it is not often challenged' (p. 28). Given the methods available for challenging an arrest, this is hardly surprising. The opportunities are limited: one may challenge the arrest in the course of a trial, one may take out a civil action or one may lodge a complaint against the police under the 1964 Police Act. But most cases do not come to trial since most defendants plead guilty (whether they believe themselves guilty or not)[4] and the legitimacy or otherwise of the arrest is therefore never challenged. Even where a case does come to trial, for a petty offence of this sort it would be likely to be before a magistrates' court and since in England at least[5] most defendants there are unrepresented (only 19 per cent are represented throughout, according to Bottoms and McClean, 1976 , p. 137) and unversed in law, there would be little chance of a challenge being made. What is more, even defendants who are represented may find their lawyer advising against questioning police conduct since it might turn the judge against him (Baldwin and McConville, 1977).[6] A civil suit is costly and legal aid is limited, and complaints against the police are rarely effective. Box and Russell (1975) show that only 18 per cent were found—by the police—to be substantiated. The improbability of successfully challenging an arrest, particularly for a trivial offence, provides one immediate reason for the ease of marginal arrests.

If challenged, however, an arrest is accountable on two aspects: first, on whether there is enough evidence to charge the suspect under a specific law with a specific offence, since an arrest must be accompanied by a charge (*Chalmers* v. *H.M.Adv.*, 1954); and second, on whether it is necessary to arrest, in the sense of keeping him in custody after the charge rather than releasing him on bail until he comes to court.

The legality of custody is defined in terms of reasonableness or the interests of justice (Renton and Brown, 1972, p. 30), neither of which sets the parameters very clearly, allowing wide scope for subjective discretion. Indeed, the common law merely offers a *post hoc* check on the 'reasonableness' of the policeman's *belief* that arrest was justified. The law also accepts the belief that people ought to be taken into custody if they have a past record (*Carlin* v. *Malloch*, 1896) or are jobless or homeless. Lord Deas, in *Peggie* v. *Clark* (1868) made it clear that the arrest of a member of 'the criminal classes' or of someone with no means of honest livelihood or fixed abode is easier to justify than that of someone who:

> even although expressly charged with a crime by an aggrieved party, be a well-known householder—a person of respectability—what, in our judicial practice, we call a 'law-abiding party'.

This statement by a judge in 1868 remains the criterion today
(Renton and Brown, 1972, p. 2). What is more, the requirement in
Scots, though not in English law, of a cash deposit for bail rather
than just a promise that the money will be paid if the accused fails to
turn up in court, leads to the detention of the same type of people—
the jobless and homeless—regardless of the trivial nature of their
offence. Even the *Ludlow* v. *Shelton* case, which found for the
complainant in his action against the police for abuse of their powers
of arrest and search and is full of civil rights rhetoric, nonetheless
draws its indignation from the *status* of the citizen so affronted: 'Is it
easy to imagine a more gross indignity offered to a perfectly
innocent and respectable professional gentleman?' (1938).

Note the parallels in law with the practical grounds for arrests
used informally by Skolnick's policeman, that the homeless or
jobless were most likely to abscond, with King's account (1971) of
police objections to bail (the two most frequently mentioned were
that the accused had previous convictions or no fixed abode) and
with Cain's account of the arrest of vagrants. In two police stations
she found that 20 per cent and 27 per cent respectively of those
arrested for marginal offences were of no fixed abode. She links this
to their vulnerability as 'a small exposed and powerless section of the
population' who are therefore particularly at risk to the policeman's
interests in making arrests, especially during 'the long cold haul
between supper break and dawn' (Cain, 1971, pp. 74–5). But it is
not just informal motivations and assessments that are involved,
subverting equality before the law. Given the law's attitude to the
homeless and jobless we could not expect equality anyway.
Pragmatics and rationalisations at the informal level—with the
consequence, intended or otherwise, of class and racial bias—are
also endorsed in formal law.

As for having sufficient evidence on a specific offence, there is also
plenty of scope for legally circumventing that principle. The specific
offence may itself be rather unspecific: breach of the peace (whose
peace?), loitering with intent or being on premises for unlawful
purposes (how does one determine purpose or intent?), possessing
goods for which one cannot satisfactorily account (how many
people carry receipts and what is satisfactory?), carrying imple-
ments that could be used for housebreaking (where does one draw
the line?), or as weapons. Even an empty milk bottle has been
defined as a dangerous weapon (Armstrong and Wilson, 1973). If
the police operate at this level with wide discretion (Bottomley,

1973) it is not just because they surreptitiously take it into their own hands but because they are formally allocated discretion on what constitutes an offence via vague substantive laws and wide procedural powers.

So, in vague cases like breach of the peace, the offence exists *because* the police say they observed someone loitering, drunk, 'bawling, shouting, cursing and swearing', to quote the daily menu for the district courts, or more unusually but nonetheless an observed case, 'jumping on and off the pavement in a disorderly fashion' (Case 30). These offences may be, in Maureen Cain's term, marginal. They are, as described, amazingly trivial. But they are also numerically significant (76 per cent of the arrests Cain (1971) observed), hence her interest in probing the non-legal reasons for police making such arrests (p. 74). But what is also important is the formal structure which makes such arrests, whatever their motivation, legal.

Likewise, one must refer to more than informal stereotyping to explain the arrest of two young boys (Case 9), a 'known thief' and his companion, who, according to the police evidence, were 'touching car handles'. Whatever the motivation of the police, the legality of their action is indisputable and the stereotyping more than informal. The General Powers Act 1960 lays down the law that known or reputed thieves in suspicious circumstances are subject to arrest. A known thief is someone with a previous conviction for dishonesty: previous convictions become therefore not just informal leads for narrowing-down suspects on committed crimes but legal grounds for arresting them. A reputed thief is someone who keeps bad company and has no known means of honest livelihood: stereotyping and assuming the worst are thus written into the law. Suspicious circumstances are left to the police to define. Thus police evidence in this case is expressed purely as subjective interpretation:

'they were touching them *as though to* open them . . .',
'he *seemed to say* to Craig to stand back . . .',
'they *appeared to be* watching and waiting . . .' (My emphasis).

Note that it is not just police practice but the formal law here which deviates from the ideals of legality, replacing arrest for a specified offence with arrest on suspicion or for prevention; replacing established law with arbitrary definitions; replacing the doctrine of trying each case on its merits with the relevance of previous convictions. Personal and bureaucratic motivations can explain why the police want to make arrests; the law itself explains why they may.

What is more, judicial sanctions on police arrests at this level are meaningless. Vague laws and wide powers effectively sidestep standards of legality and proof by equating the subjective police decision with substantive law and requisite evidence. The police are given the statutory powers to define the limits of the behaviour that constitutes public order. It is not necessary to prove any ill effect, for example, in a breach of the peace, that anyone was offended or even affected: a breach has occurred:

> where something is done in breach of public order or decorum which *might reasonably be expected* to lead to the lieges being alarmed or upset. . . . (*Raffaeli* v. *Heatly*, 1949; my emphasis)

So the refusal of members of the public to say they were offended in witnessing the incident, a point regularly made in police reports, is rendered irrelevant, as indeed judges point out to juries, reading out the legal definitions and emphasising: 'Note that 'might be'. There need not be evidence that anyone was actually upset' (Case 93). Nor is there any need to prove intent in cases like these, by, for example, reference to:

> any particular act or acts tending to show the purpose or intent; he may be convicted if, from the circumstances of the case and from his known character, the court is of the opinion that he was intending to commit a felony. (Vagrancy Act 1824, s. 12)

No further evidence than the policeman's general statement of his impression unsubstantiated even by details of how he formed it seems to be required. Hence Case 29 where the accused were convicted of attempted theft from cars:

Prosecutor:    And was anything missing?
Policeman:    No. They didn't get in.
Prosecutor:    But you are sure they were trying to get in?
Policeman:    The behaviour of the boys left me in no doubt that they were trying to enter the van.

Indeed statutory offences involving intent need not even specify what the accused was intending to do. According to *Phillips* v. *Heatly* (1964):

> where an accused person is charged under an Act making it an offence to loiter with intent to, or to be found about to, commit an arrestable offence . . . it is sufficient to aver in the complaint that he was intending or about to commit 'an arrestable offence' and unnecessary to specify which offence he is alleged to have contemplated. (Renton and Brown, 1972, p. 203)

Indeed in some public order offences there need not even be evidence that the accused was doing or intending to do anything, merely being part of an offensive crowd is enough. Hence Case 30, where the charge was breach of the peace, involving 'jumping on and off a pavement in a disorderly fashion', and the accused was the only one of a small group of youths who pleaded not guilty. His independent defence was that he was not doing anything, the lads had called to him as he was passing and he merely stopped to say hello, he 'didn't like to pass them by'. The prosecutor's cross-examination was directed not at what he was doing but that he was *there*, something he readily agreed to:

Accused:      I didn't run off because I didn't expect to be lifted . . .

But the prosecutor pressed the point:

Prosecutor:     He admits he was there quarter of an hour or so [an exaggeration of the testimony]. It's all relative of course so he may think he wasn't misbehaving as much as the others *but he stayed with them*. (My emphasis).

And that, as it emerged, was all that was necessary in law:

Assessor:     Mr S. I want to make it clear that if you're with people who are misbehaving the law is that if you stay with them you're involved. It may be a technical offence in this instance but you've got to keep away from people like this or you're tarred with the same brush.

Case 2 demonstrates the same legal situation:

> Policeman:     I can't identify individuals except those two but they were all part of an aggressive group.

The law in marginal offences leaves very little to be proved, and since the offence presupposes a specified offender 'caught red-handed at the scene of the crime' and eye-witnesses, there is nothing left at issue but the credibility of the police versus the accused. Indeed given the openness of the law the police scarcely need to lie about the grounds for arrest: at least that is the import of the prosecutor's cross-examination in Case 29. The accused maintained that the police had made up the story of touching car handles in order to take them to the police station to investigate a case of stolen television sets. They were 'stalling for time'. The prosecutor indignantly declared it quite incredible that the police would have made up such a story

> because they couldn't get you for anything else. . . . They could have charged you with playing football in the street and they wouldn't need to have made it up. (Case 29)

Little wonder that in court arrest becomes synonymous with guilt:

> Policeman:     [in the face of denial by the accused] You did or you wouldn't have been apprehended . . .
> Prosecutor:     You weren't shouting and swearing?
> Accused:     No sir.
> Prosecutor:     Then how do you explain why you're here? (Case 13)

> Policeman:     If anyone hadn't been aggressive he wouldn't have been there. (Case 2)

In Scotland corroboration is required to meet the standards of legal sufficiency[7] but since the police (as a result of this legal requirement rather than the hostility of the natives) frequently go around in pairs, this is rarely a problem.

The magistrate who sums up 'I see no reason to disbelieve the police' (Case 8) is not informally ignoring his right to sanction police behaviour but recognising that there is at law nothing to sanction.

The openness of the law gives wide scope for legitimate arrest and few grounds for judicial control.What is more, in the nature of the case there is no such category as a suspect and no such process as investigation, only the encounter between the policeman and the accused, and since most of the ideology of civil rights focuses on the police–suspect relationship in the course of investigation there is little to take issue with, or protection from, there. It is hardly surprising then that marginal behaviour dominates police work and, since less marginal cases requiring harder proof are more likely to be dropped in the early stages (Mack, 1976) it is not surprising that trivial cases dominate the courts even more. In petty offences judicial control of the police is abrogated by the law.

For the minor offences which dominate the courts incrimination is not a problem either practically or legally. Indeed the three analytical stages of incrimination, assembling a case, and convincing the court collapse into one. The policeman's observations constitute the grounds for arrest, the substance of the case, and the authoritative presentation to convince the magistrate. There is little at issue for the court to decide in its role of reaching a verdict—nor indeed for it to control in its role of watchdog on the police.

It may not be surprising that the tendency of sociologists to concentrate on this vague kind of offence where police discretion is so wide has meant in turn so much emphasis on the operation of discretion, rather than the legal structure in which it takes place. But it is very much a structurally provided discretion, a legal power, that is involved, and it is not the only type of offence that has to be dealt with.

The opposite case is one where everything is at issue, the classic detective story where an offence is reported, the offender has to be traced from 'clues' and evidence for a case established by search and questioning. It is here that the clash between crime control and civil rights comes into play. The job of incrimination in 'real crime' is much more significant, and one of the difficulties the police pinpoint is that the law itself 'gives virtually no assistance to the police and every assistance to a suspect wishing to hide his guilt'.[8]

But this is where it becomes important to tease out the substance not just of crime but of law. For if we examine the law in greater detail we find a spider's web of distinctions and exceptions which present a quite different picture of the legal relationship of police and suspect: police powers of arrest and search are far more extensive than the rhetoric suggests; detention for questioning can be a legitimate activity; the right to silence can be less a *right* and a hurdle to conviction than a *fact* that facilitates it.

## ARREST

Arrest—that is, the detention of a person against his will—may be legally carried out only in relation to a specified offence. Otherwise attendance at the police station is purely voluntary. This is the spirit of the Judges' Rules. Barry Cox (1975) points out succinctly the gap between this ideology and practice:

> Detention for questioning is therefore in theory impossible; in practice 'helping the police with their inquiries' is a daily event. (p. 172)

How is this possible? Partly because of the simple fact that if such arrest is impossible in theory it is nonetheless perfectly possible in *law*. Although they are much referred to as a symbol of legality, the Judges' Rules are *not* law, only principles for administrative guidance. Authoritative law on arrest is rather different.

For example, the *voluntary* nature of helping the police with their inquiries has been interpreted in law, to say the least, very widely. Consider the Scottish case of *Swankie* v. *Milne* in 1973 which defines the current situation. This was deemed not only not to be an *illegal* arrest but not to be an arrest at all. The judges accepted that the police had stopped the accused in his car, taken his keys away, waited with him and would have prevented him from leaving if he had tried to. However, they concluded that the accused had remained voluntarily and had not therefore been arrested. What their judgement would have been if he had tried to leave is unclear. But it is also an arrestable offence according to the 1964 Police Act to obstruct the police in the execution of their duty, and this has been interpreted as 'the doing of any act which makes it more difficult for the police to carry out their duty' (*Rice* v. *Connolly*, 1966). What precisely that means remains an open question. Although Lord Justice Parker in the same case refuted the idea that refusing to answer questions, even allied with a generally obstructive and sarcastic attitude, was *not* obstructing a policeman in his duty. Justice James made a point of noting that:

I would not go so far as to say there may not be circumstances in which the manner of a person together with his silence could amount to an obstruction within the section; whether it does remains to be decided in any case that happens hereafter, not in this case, in which it has not been argued. (*Rice* v. *Connolly*, 1966)

It becomes rather difficult to see how someone can avoid being arrested if the police have a mind to arrest him. Furthermore, refusing to co-operate is not a far cry from resistance, which is, of course, an arrestable offence; nor is resistance far from another offence, assault.

Indeed, in court, resisting arrest tends to be presented by prosecutors as indicative of guilt and therefore a justification of the arrest on the first charge anyway. 'Only the guilty take advantage of civil rights' is the line taken. On the other hand, with the nice skill lawyers have of always holding the winning trick, failing to resist is also suspicious. Witness Case 8.

The prosecutor was suggesting that the accused *must* have been guilty or he would not have allowed himself to have been seized (uncharged) by two men (the police were in plain clothes) without resisting:

| | |
|---|---|
| Prosecutor: | You didn't do anything? |
| Accused: | I couldn't. |
| Prosecutor: | You didn't say 'What are you doing?' |
| Accused: | No, it was all too quick. |
| Prosecutor: | And no explanation was given at all? |
| Accused: | No. |
| Prosecutor: | When did you gather they were policemen? |
| Accused: | I asked them—they said they were taking me to the station. |
| Prosecutor: | But why assume they were policemen? There *are* railway stations. |

In his summing up the prosecutor considered it doubly suspicious that the accused's companion had not fought off the two policemen if his friend was being innocently seized:

| | |
|---|---|
| Prosecutor: | According to his story, his companion made no protest while the accused was dragged out by two unknown men. This is quite incredible. He is clearly guilty of this charge. |

The companion in question might, however, have been relieved that he had *not* intervened if he had heard the accused's mother's account of her night in jail charged with breach of the peace when she went to protest, or if he had witnessed Case 13:

> Policeman:    One youth ran towards us saying 'What are you taking him in for? It's a fucking liberty. He's done fuck all!' He was cautioned and charged with breach of the peace.

In any case, the prosecutor's argument was only about the credibility of the accused not the legality of the arrest. Indeed, in cases of resistance or assault, even if the arrest was unfounded and illegal it is still, in English law, 'open to the jury to convict of common assault' (Halsbury, 1969, vol. 25, p. 364) and the charge sticks even if the resister did not know the person seizing him was a policeman. In short, the law itself does not encourage standing on one's right to freedom from arbitrary arrest.

Given this, the warrant system provides a potential method for safeguarding the citizen against *arbitrary* arrest since it involves a specific charge and acceptance by a neutral judge that there are grounds for suspecting the accused. Of course, not everyone demands to see a warrant when he is arrested or even knows he may—the lower his status, indeed, the less likely he is to demand evidence of authority. And this fits with the familiar theory that rights available in law, be they on civil liberties or welfare entitlements, fail in practice because citizens do not take them up. The law itself is thus exonerated. But that may be a little misleading. Indeed there is some evidence that the very fact of rights being taken up can itself become a reason for removing them. The Thompson Committee (1975), for example, notes:

> . . . the police at present are able to carry out their functions only because some persons whom they detain without warrant fail, through ignorance, or fear of authority, to exercise their rights. (p. 11)

However they also note that:

> As people become increasingly aware of their rights the present tacit co-operation which makes it possible for the police to

function may not continue, and the police may find themselves in a position to do only what they are specifically authorised to do by law. (p. 12)

—which of course is exactly what legality means! But legality is presented here less as an ideal than a problem: the solution is not to support this claiming of rights or take further measures to ensure all suspects *do* know their rights *but to remove the rights* by introducing 'a form of limited, or temporary arrest, arrest on suspicion' (Thomson Committee, 1975, p. 12), with a different name—detention—and more relaxed rules. In short they recommend police powers be widened so that they do not need a warrant, not only in practice, but in law.

In any case police powers are already wider than the warrant system might suggest. In *R.* v. *Kulynycz* (1971) it was agreed that arresting without a warrant while pretending to have one was not fatal to the case; the Criminal Law Act 1967 allows a member of the public or a policeman to arrest without warrant 'anyone who is, or whom he reasonably suspects to be in the act of committing an arrestable offence'; while a policeman may also arrest someone whom he reasonably suspects is *about* to commit an arrestable offence. So in most serious cases a suspect can be arrested without warrant. Specific Acts often have specific powers of arrest without warrant attached, e.g. in drug offences, immigration offences, and motoring offences. Under Scots law, the police may arrest without warrant for all common law crimes (most crimes being based on common law) and for statutory offences, categories which can cover most incidents.

Warrants of course affect not just arrest but search. However, searching a suspect for evidence without a warrant is generally excused if the police plead 'urgency', 'urgency being widely interpreted in favour of the police' (Rentôn and Brown, 1972, p. 36; *Bell* v. *Hogg*, 1967; *Hay* v. *H.M.Adv.*, 1968). Indeed even the seizure without warrant of perfectly legitimate goods has been deemed acceptable in English law. In *Chic Fashions* v. *Jones*, 1968 Lord Justice Salmon pointed out that the police had reasonable grounds to suspect that the goods seized might be stolen, and since in the law of arrest 'reasonable grounds to suspect' legitimises seizure of the *person*, he could scarcely hold that the same did not apply to mere *property*:

If a man's person is not so sacrosanct in the eyes of the law, how can the goods which he is reasonably suspected of having stolen or received be sacrosanct? Only if the law regards property as more important than liberty and I do not accept that it does so.

Common law thus managed to justify invading personal liberty to recover property by the principle that personal liberty is more significant in law than property. In doing so of course it set up a new precedent that reversed its own justification, making the right to recover *possibly* stolen property outweigh the right to individual freedom from interference from the police.

In any case, the control function of the warrant seems rendered redundant by the view expressed in the authoritative Scots manual on procedure that 'such petitions, being presented by responsible officials, are assumed to be well-founded' (Renton and Brown, 1972, p. 28). This is rather at odds with Lord Hewart's rhetoric on the rule of law over officials too:

> One of our most priceless possessions is the liberty of the subject. If once we show any signs of giving way to the abominable doctrine that because things are done by officials, some immunity must be extended to them, what is to become of our country? (*Ludlow* v. *Shelton* 1938)

However, the view that officials can be trusted was upheld by the Thomson Committee (1975) in the face of requests for change and it was on this basis that they found it 'satisfactory' for judges to 'rubber stamp' rather than investigate requests for warrants (p. 20). Lafave and Remington's American study of the warrant system (1975) points to informal judicial laxness as the source of its ineffectiveness, but from these views expounded by a legal authority and a committee set up by the government and Crown Office and chaired by a High Court Judge, it would seem in the Scottish case to be formally endorsed common law and policy.

Detaining someone is not then in general quite so hampered by controls as one might imagine from the rhetoric. Nor, more specifically, is detention for questioning. In the case of *R.* v. *Houghton*, 1978, Lord Justice Lawton said that:

> except under the Prevention of Terrorism (Temporary Powers) Act 1976, the police had no power to arrest anyone so that they could make inquiries about him.

Indeed the combination of rules on arrest—no arrest without a charge—and the rules on interrogation—no interrogation after charge, would seem to render it legally impossible. But there are ways round this: one is the holding charge. The rules prohibiting interrogation in custody refer only to interrogation about the offence with which the person has already been charged. There is no rule against using one charge to take a person into custody then interrogating him in the isolation of the police station on another offence. The holding charge thus allows a suspect to be questioned in private and in custody until a confession is elicited. It also opens the way for search. Search of someone's person or home is not permissible in order to find evidence unless there are prior grounds for suspecting him of an offence. 'An Englishman's home is his castle' is indeed an old legal maxim expressing the prohibition on search without warrant. But the holding charge obviates this. Once arrested, the person, and the premises he is in, can be legally searched, and if evidence relevant to another charge is unearthed, the search is quite lawful and the evidence admissible.

In short, according to case law the police may with impunity make an arbitrary arrest, arresting not on a charge based on some kind of proof of specific implication in a specific offence, but arresting in order to acquire that proof or find out if there has been any activity that could be defined as an offence. ('That could be defined' is important. Remember we are not always talking about finding sacks marked 'Swag', but, for example, political posters and pamphlets.) Authoritative common law thus unceremoniously turns the basic principle governing arrest on its head.

Wide police discretion over petty offences thus takes on further significance. Defining as arrestable offences behaviour as indeterminate as intent, loitering, or breach of the peace, a known thief in suspicious circumstances and so on gives the police wide powers of legal detention, and these powers may be used to establish evidence for a different suspected offence, which the policeman is really interested in but has no evidence on which to charge and therefore arrest. Remember Case 29, the case of the irrelevant television,[9] in which according to the evidence of the defendants, it was exactly this motivation that prompted the police to invoke the General Powers Act to arrest them. They tried to use this point to lend credibility to their story that they were 'lifted' for nothing, that they 'were not touching cars' but 'playing football and he came up and asked us about a TV set'.

Magistrate:      Look, this charge is nothing to do with a stolen
                 television. You're doing yourself no good telling
                 me   you're   involved   in   another   charge.
                 Understand?

But, of course, the suspicion of involvement with a stolen television
set might have had everything to do with the use of the holding
charge and be absolutely relevant to the defendant's alleged
innocence. The police may indeed drop both the holding charge
and the other case so that the chance to raise the matter in court at
all is denied unless the defendant takes out a suit for wrongful arrest.

The Judges' Rules specify as an overriding principle and
fundamental condition that only voluntary statements are
admissible, with a veto on questioning after charge precisely in
recognition of the unreliability of 'confessions' in such
circumstances. So the holding charge is quite contrary to the whole
underlying spirit of the Rules. But it is perfectly legal. Renton and
Brown (1972) point out indeed:

> The police could presumably arrest an offender on this charge
> and hold him until they obtained a warrant on the charge in
> which they were really interested. (p. 32)

The distinction between questioning in custody on the offence
charged and questioning in custody for another offence was
recognised as a problem in the 1930 Judges' Rules, but it was still
left as a loophole in the 1964 version. Not an overlooked loophole
though, for case law positively supports it. In R. v. Buchan, 1964, the
judge specifically used the loophole in the Judges' Rules to justify
police questioning on a possible burglary charge after arrest on a
vague loitering charge. The case of Christie v. Leachinsky, 1947, is
often cited as upholding a person's right to be told why he is being
arrested. But like many cases it is double-edged since Lord
Simmonds also declared that it could not

> be wrongful to arrest and detain a man upon a charge, of which
> he is reasonably suspected, with a view to further investigation of
> a second charge upon which information is incomplete.

Indeed he went on to assert:

... it is not an essential condition of lawful arrest that the constable should at the time of arrest formulate any charge at all, much less the charge which may ultimately be found in the indictment.

Detention for questioning is thus legally endorsed. Holding charge practices do not require abuse but simply use of the law. They are not informal subversions of due process: they are due process as defined by common law and statute.

## HELPING THE POLICE WITH THEIR INQUIRIES

However, interrogation of suspects, interrogation in custody and without caution is legal in much broader terms. The Judges' Rules refer to questioning in custody before charge:

> When a police officer is trying to discover whether, or by whom, an offence has been committed he is entitled to question any person whether suspected or not from whom he thinks that useful information may be obtained. This is so whether or not the person has been taken into custody so long as he has not been charged with the offence or informed that he may be prosecuted for it. (Rule I)

In cases like *Chandler* (1976) in England, *Aitken* (1926) or *Chalmers* (1954) in Scotland, all dealing specifically with police questioning, the judges explicitly discuss the situation of the accused who is being questioned in custody without being cautioned. But if the judges have required that a person cannot be taken into custody unless he is cautioned and charged or told why, (*Christie* v *Leachinsky*, 1947) and insisted in Rule IIIb of the Judges' Rules that once charged a person should normally no longer be questioned, how can they also discuss in leading cases the questioning of an accused person in custody?

The situation reflected in the blatant contradiction in the Judges' Rules has been achieved by the gradual refinements and vacillating metaphors of legal reasoning by which the judges have established a limbo, sitting uneasily between the law of arrest and the law of interrogation.

The protection offered by the principles of arrest and interrogation outlined above depends on a two-stage model of police–citizen relations. One is either a citizen entitled to his freedom from arrest or the accused who, with a prima facie case against him, can be charged and if necessary taken into custody. The two-stage model reflects a once clearly defined structural distinction whereby the magistrates took over after arrest and any questioning was done in court under the supervision of the court, not the people reporting or investigating the offence. This gradually changed with the introduction in the early nineteenth century of an organised police force, followed by the development of detection, widening of police powers, and changes in the accused's legal situation in court. The gap that has developed between ideology and legal practice is thus a reflection of a changing structure but a lingering rhetoric. Nonetheless the two stages were being strictly adhered to by English judges at the end of the nineteenth century, so in *R. v. Gavin* (1885) the judge stated categorically:

> When a person is in custody the police have no right to ask him questions. . . . A prisoner's mouth is closed after he is once given the charge, and he ought not to be asked anything. (1885: 15 Cox C.C.)

Note the interchangeability of the points of 'custody' and 'charge' with the implication that custody could not take place without charge.

But in more recent cases the judges have operated in their decisions on the legitimacy of police control with a *three-stage* model of investigation which distinguishes the point of custody from the point of charge and in which the first category is governed by the law of arrest, the third by the law of interrogation but the second avoids both. The three-stage model is implicit in the English Judges' Rules, made particularly clear by the addition in the 1964 version of a second caution. Early in the inquiry the individual is classified as a *citizen* helping police with their inquiries, next he becomes a (possibly) cautioned *suspect*, and finally when there is enough prima facie evidence, *the* cautioned and charged *accused*. Both English and Scots common law spell out the same model, exemplified in England by *R. v. Osbourne and Virtue* (1973), in Scotland by *Bell* v. *H.M.Adv.* (1945). Only at the *third stage* does a prohibition on interrogation become applicable. The proud boast of Scots law that 'the law is very jealous of the rights of the *charged* prisoner' thus takes on both a significant and a hollow ring (Renton and Brown, 1972,

p. 382; my emphasis). Interrogation of the *suspect* in custody has been interpreted since the *Ibrahim* case of 1914 as undesirable but nonetheless legal.

The net result is that protection from interrogation is available only at a very late stage in the process—only in fact after enough evidence is available for a charge—and it is procedurally defined out at the crucial early stages of establishing incriminating evidence for that charge. The law thus, by neatly pigeonholing points and conditions where its rules apply, creates the opportunity for extensive legal police interrogation in custody.

Given this position in law the situational definition of the point at which the individual or suspect becomes the accused is vital for claiming rights or raising issues of admissibility. And obviously such defining is a fluid and subjective process. Nevertheless the judges, when faced with the question of narrowing down the accused's rights, have managed to divide it into three definite logical stages. When it comes to defining the point at which those rights come into play, however, a new metaphor for characterising social reality is employed. The situation is suddenly revealed as not a three-stage structure but a fluid process, and the crucial point is left vague and almost mystically elusive:

> Just when that point of time is reached is in any particular case extremely difficult to define—or even for an experienced police officer to realise its arrival. There does come a time, however, when a police officer carrying out his duty honestly and conscientiously, ought to be in a position to appreciate that the man whom he is in process of questioning is under serious consideration as the perpetrator of the crime. Once that stage of suspicion is reached, the suspect is in the position that thereafter the only evidence admissible against him is his own voluntary statement. (*Chalmers* v. *H.M.Adv.*, 1954)

The timing is thus left for definition to the police themselves, the people with the most obvious vested interest in postponing the point of inadmissibility as long as possible.

Indeed Scots law to some extent acknowledges the unprotected position of the suspect. Hence Lord Anderson's view in *H.M.Adv.* v *Aitken* (1926) that the suspect ought to have protection of some sort too:

Now it seems to me that the court ought to be more jealous to safeguard the rights of a prisoner in a case where a charge has not yet been made, but where the prisoner has merely been detained by the police on suspicion.

But the safeguard introduced is operated by two criteria, one too broad and one, ironically, too narrow to provide a clear statement of what is legitimate police conduct. The substantive criterion is 'fairness to the accused', too broad in substance to specify any meaning, and the operative criterion to bring this into play is each case's 'own specific circumstances', too particular to allow generalisation from one case to another. Together they indicate neatly how the intrinsic specificity of the case law method allied to the common law habit of declaration of broad principles rather than tight rulings, leads to grand civil rights rhetoric but plenty of scope for discretionary judicial practice.

Linking the concept of fairness to a specific case with *multiple circumstances* involved makes it difficult to call on any *one* of these circumstances as a precedent establishing a criterion for inadmissibility—so despite the rhetoric expressed in this case of the need for safeguards for the suspect, it could not be said to establish them. As Renton and Brown (1972) coyly put it:

> The fact that the accused had been a suspect was, however, only one circumstance among a number which led his Lordship to reject the statement made by him to the police. (p. 375)

The other circumstances indicate rather that the idea applies to unusual rather than average situations: the accused in the *Aitken* case was under seventeen, sick and mentally subnormal. The implication is therefore that there is nothing essentially unfair about interrogation in custody of a normal adult suspect. In any case in *Chalmers* v. *H.M.Adv* (1954) and in *Miln* v. *Cullen* (1967) 'fairness', introduced to protect the accused, took on a new twist—fairness meant not merely fairness to the accused but to the public interest and to the police in doing their job. In judicial reasoning the words can remain constant but the meanings change—one reason for the divergence between the rhetoric and the reality of law.

In both systems, of course, the suspect should be cautioned, warned of the danger of incriminating himself, but common law qualifies that by accepting that failure to caution does not necessarily make the evidence inadmissible (*Jeffrey* v. *Black*, 1977), while in any case the caution may well be seen as a mere formality in a situation where the police can detain and question the accused in the privacy of the police station. The suspect category thus provides a neat limbo between the uncharged citizen who can be questioned but not in custody and the accused who can be taken into custody but should not generally be questioned on the details of the incident.

If this situation has been established by the judges, though, it has also been questioned by them. In the significant *Chalmers* case—significant to lawyers because the appeal court of three judges not only quashed the conviction but deemed the issues raised important enough to be adjourned for consideration by the full bench of eight—the Lord Justice General recognised the divergence of this situation from the rhetoric:

> . . . no person can be lawfully detained except after a charge has been made against him, and it is for this reason that I view with some uneasiness the situation disclosed in this case and illustrated by the recent cases of *Rigg* and *Short*, in which a suspect is neither apprehended nor charged but is simply 'asked' to accompany two police officers to a police office to be there questioned. (1954 J.C.)

But this uneasiness did *not* make itself felt in a dictum prohibiting the practice. It would thus seem to be more of a gesture to the rhetoric which—however strongly felt—nonetheless upholds the limbo of interrogation in custody—an example indeed of how judicial ambivalence serves to bridge or at least blur the gap between the rhetoric and reality of law. Later cases have made this implicit acceptance of interrogation in custody quite explicit. In *Miln* v. *Cullen* (1967), for example, Lord Wheatley welcomed the case as 'an opportunity for clearing up certain misapprehensions which may have arisen in the minds of the legal profession, the police and the public' as a result of *Chalmers*. Questioning a suspect in custody was legitimate, indeed, was what the caution suggested, while fairness meant not only fairness to the accused but to the public; the courts should be seeking a balance, not 'hamstringing the police in their investigation of crime with a series of academic vetoes which ignore the realities and practicalities of the situation and discount completely the public interest' (1967).

In short it is not just the police who take the law into their own hands in detaining people in custody to 'help with their inquiries'.

Nor indeed is it just the police who informally point to the practical needs of crime control to justify ignoring the principles of legality: that same justification is writ large and indeed offered as guidance for the police, in the cases, textbooks and government reports which formulate the law itself. Police justifications may be a distortion of the spirit of legality but they are an exact replica of the spirit of the law.

## VOLUNTARY STATEMENTS

The implication of the three-stage model is that once a charge is made questioning about the offence stops. In short, the nineteenth-century common law prohibition still holds: it is simply redefined to come into play at a later point. But the absoluteness of even that prohibition has also been diluted over time. In both Scots and English law the crucial condition for admitting evidence has become not so much when the evidence was acquired but how it was provided.

The absolute prohibition on questioning in custody expressed in late nineteenth-century English cases like *R.* v. *Gavin* and *R.* v. *Male and Cooper* put the emphasis very much on the danger implicit in the privacy of the police station with no-one present to see how the matter was conducted. This echoes very much the fear on which civil liberties ideology was originally based, with the common law growing up in the wake of interrogation by torture in the King's Court of Star Chamber, and a consequent emphasis on receiving only *voluntary* statements as evidence in court. Prohibiting questioning in custody at all, the idea that still comes through in the broad principles governing investigation, was clearly one extreme means of allaying those fears. Any statements made in response to questioning in custody were basically treated as involuntary. This definition of voluntary and involuntary statements however did not last long and the *Ibrahim* v. *R.* case of 1914 dismissed it as *not the law*. Whether a person in custody was asked questions or not was not the crux of the issue and never had been. What mattered in law was simply whether the answer was given voluntarily, 'in the sense that it has not been obtained from him by fear of prejudice or hope of advantage. . . . The principle is as old as Lord Hale.' This remains the law in England today.

Scotland stuck much longer to the view that there should be no questioning after the charge and that anything said in custody should be treated with suspicion (e.g. *H.M.Adv.* v. *Rigg*, 1946) but a similar gradual change has occurred there too. In 1938 the judges were still declaring:

> It is a statutory rule, which ought to be observed in the future, when a prisoner has been committed for further inquiry, that the police ought not to approach him on any question touching the crime with which he has been charged. (*Stark and Smith* v. *H.M.Adv.*, 1938).

But by 1966 Lord Cameron could state:

> I know of no authoritative decision in the law of Scotland which lays down that once a person has become a suspect he may not therefore be questioned by the police at all, or that if they do question him the answers which he makes may not be given in evidence. (*Brown* v. *H.M.Adv.*)

And by 1967 Lord Wheatley was expressing a view, which ironically used the criteria introduced in the *Aitken* case to *protect* the *suspect* who was not protected by the three-stage model, but used it to *dilute* the protection offered by the three-stage model to the *charged accused*: 'It is wrong to assume that after a person has been cautioned and charged questioning of that person is no longer admissible.' (*Miln* v. *Cullen*). Rather admissibility depends on the fairness of the circumstances. Thus can precedents be decontextualised and used for purposes diametrically opposed to their original intent.

There is therefore no longer a prohibition as such on questioning after charge. Rather the voluntariness of statements made by the suspect or accused to the police, in response to questions or not, is assessed in terms of whether or not they were acquired by inducement or oppression. In these terms there is fairly wide scope for defining confessions or other incriminating statements by the accused as voluntary. So admissions secured by bugging cells, tapping phones at the police station (the judge pointed out that the policeman had not said he would not listen) or by a policeman in plain clothes posing as a prisoner have all been admitted in England as the accused's voluntary statements (Leigh, 1975, pp. 165, 157), while what a prisoner was overheard saying to his wife has been allowed as evidence against him despite the rules against hearsay, against a

wife being forced to testify against her husband, and despite the
rhetoric against self-incrimination (Cross, 1974, p. 475). In Scotland intercepted letters and conversations in prison between
prisoners and between a man and his visiting brother have all been
admitted (Walker and Walker, 1975, p. 37).

Indeed literally the reasoning is quite accurate. The information
in question may well have been volunteered by the accused but *not*
with any intention to volunteer it *to the police*. By focusing on the
meaning of the word rather than setting it in the context of the
purpose of the rule, and by ignoring the accused's subjective
intentions (despite all the normal rhetoric of 'mens rea'), judicial
reasoning thus extends the admissibility of self-incriminating
statements and the legitimate exercise of police powers. This style of
reasoning is not consistent, however. Admitting statements acquired by inducement or oppression by someone who is *not* a
policeman or other official is justified precisely by putting the action
in the context of the purpose of previous precedents: to protect the
citizen *vis-à-vis* state power in the form of the *police*. Textbook
statements of the law in Scotland all qualify these situations with the
criteria of 'fairness to the accused' but the authority cited is usually
*Aitken* and we have already seen how limited the precedent set there
is in its applicability.

The terms 'inducement' and 'oppression' are themselves of course
like 'voluntariness', not self-evident but subject to the interpretation
of the court. The law does not take account of the more subtle
aspects of the terms. Inman (1978) points out the discrepancy
between the subtle psychological methods of persuasion advocated
by police manuals, and the more blatant, objective coercion
prohibited by law. Even in these terms though, some of the
interpretations of inducement and oppression may seem rather
surprising. Questioning the accused in custody overnight for ten
hours out of seventeen, the last seven continuously, is not considered
oppressive (*R*. v. *Prager*, 1972), while the Lord Chief Justice stated
in *R*. v. *Isequilla* that:

> such considerations as fatigue, lack of sleep, emotional strain
> cannot be efficacious to deprive a confession of its quality of
> voluntariness (1975).

Decisions on inducement vary. Sometimes it is defined broadly to
favour the accused. For example appeals have been won because of

inducements as mild as a policeman saying 'I think it would be better if you made a statement telling me exactly what happened' (*R*. v. *Richards*, 1967). However the House of Lords (*D.P.P.* v. *Ping Lin*, 1976) has now decided that inducement alone does not constitute involuntariness and therefore result in automatic inadmissibility, that it is a factual matter for the court to decide. The argument is that a confession after inducement may be produced not because of it but despite it.

One major induced confession that is always allowed is 'Queen's evidence', where one accused is induced to 'confess' and incriminate another in return for the biggest inducement of all, his freedom despite his acknowledged guilt. The lawbooks simply do not discuss Queen's evidence in relation to the issue of inducement and voluntariness at all but it is not logically distinct from it. An even more blatant omission is the fact that there is in law a sentence discount for pleading guilty. What stronger inducement to incriminate oneself could there be? Rhetoric and reality are held together here only by the subcategorisations of legal knowledge, distinguishing the inadmissibility of evidence from the law on sentencing although the principles and effects are the same.

Where a statement is spontaneous—that is, not in reply to a question, threat or inducement—it is always declared voluntary and admissible. So for example anything said by the accused in reply to being cautioned is always accepted as incriminating evidence. It has been so defined since *R*.v. *Baldry*, (1852) and the logic is irrefutable. After all he has just been informed he need not speak and warned of the consequences of doing so. Of course this is one of those occasions where literal and situational logic tend to be at odds. The law on other occasions operates on the common sense assumption that accusations demand replies,[10] and this certainly seems to operate in a good many cases, despite the warning. It is as though the content of the caution is ignored and replaced by the normal cues and expectations of everyday conversation – when someone addresses a statement to you about yourself you reply, especially if you are being accused of something discreditable, especially if the other person is standing, waiting and holding a notebook, and especially if that person is someone in authority—like a policeman. Fisher (1977) suggests that even the content of the caution:

seems to assume that the person cautioned *will* speak ('whatever

you say') and if the caution is immediately followed by a question
in the form 'What do you want to say to me?' the impression will
be given to some people that they are expected, or even
requested, to speak. (p.17)

Indeed the very concept in law of 'replies to charges' seems to
recognise the implicit interrogatory nature of the charge.

A fairly crude analysis of 100 official police reports[11] which record
replies to cautions produces these statistics: 48 people are reported
as actually remaining silent or saying they had nothing to say. Of
the rest, twenty three replies were incriminating, either directly—
'I'm caught'—or indirectly by way of justification—'I was bloody
angry' or the simple, hopeful, but fatal, 'I'm sorry'. Nine were
directly discrediting or hostile to the police—'Piss off you bastards'
or 'Fucking gestapo'. Remarks like these reflecting drunkenness,
cultural hostility, or just plain anger at what seems an unjust
situation might make situational sense outside the court with the
policemen indeed giving as good as they get. But read out from the
witness box to robed and wigged dignatories in the cool rational
propriety of a trial without the context of what the police said or did
themselves—for this is how they are presented—they are quite
simply discrediting evidence.

It is not just literal and situational logic that are in contradiction
here though; accepting replies to charges as a matter of routine
contradicts other aspects of legal logic. The fact that it may be in the
interests of the police to report replies to charges in an incriminating
form does not rule them out, although statements made by the
accused favourable to himself are *not* admissible on exactly these
grounds. So in cases of rioting, the prosecution can prove that the
accused had incited others to riot, but the accused cannot lead
evidence that he advised people to have nothing to do with it
(Renton and Brown, 1972, p. 388). Replies are admissible even
where still more rules of evidence are broken, not just the rules of
hearsay and self-incrimination but also the rules on bad character;
that is, the fact that the accused has a record. Usually evidence
cannot be introduced in court for fear of prejudicing the defence
case on what is held to be irrelevant matters but replies to police
charges are always admissible even when they contain exactly that
kind of information. The classic example is the reply: 'The idea is
ridiculous. It is the big things I go in for.' (*H.M.Adv.* v. *McFadyen*,
1926).

Voluntariness as a criterion for accepting self-incriminating statements by a person accused of committing an offence does not therefore rule out quite as much information from the court as one might imagine. Questioning, inducement, threats and replies to charges have all been interpreted or admitted generously enough to allow wide scope for the use of self-incriminating statements in court. There is also a 'catch-22' involved. Voluntariness might be taken to mean that one can choose *not* to volunteer information; the irony is that remaining silent can be taken as incriminating evidence too.

## A RIGHT TO SILENCE?

The idea of a suspect's right to silence is one that turns up repeatedly in discussions of criminal procedure, particularly from police and prosecution. The Criminal Law Revision Committee of 1972 made a major issue of it, while the 1978 Royal Commission has had its share of evidence on this theme. Cases sometimes refer to the right to silence too—though they put it in inverted commas (e.g. *R.* v. *Chandler*, 1976), a stylistic reflection of the view of strict jurists that the idea of a right to silence is not a legal concept but a perversion of the legal privilege against self-incrimination. The law puts it in more negative terms: one is *not bound* to incriminate oneself; there is *no duty* to answer police questions (*Rice* v. *Connolly*, 1966). Popular rhetoric—and one might add particularly prosecution rhetoric— thus turns a negative privilege into a positive right. To lawyers the distinction is significant, with the negative statement carrying much less protection. But whichever way you look at it, the principle is contradicted by legal procedure. Having a right to silence might suggest it cannot therefore be used against you; having a privilege against self-incrimination might suggest that the very act of taking that privilege up could not therefore be used to incriminate you. Yet that is exactly what can happen in law.

For a start it depends on when you choose to exercise the right or privilege. If you refuse to answer questions before being cautioned that you need not, your silence can be taken in law to mean guilt. Lord Diplock in *Hall* v. *The Queen* (1971) confronted this by suggesting that everyone had a common law right, even before being cautioned, to stay silent on being accused of or questioned about a crime *without* the conclusion being drawn (with the inevitable qualification of exceptional circumstances) that silence means guilt. In *R.* v. *Chandler* (1976 1 W.L.R.) the trial judge reiterated this right but suggested a neat loophole in his summing up to the jury:

> You must ask yourself whether he declined to answer questions in the knowledge that he was exercising his common law right to remain silent or whether he remained silent because he might have thought if he had answered he would in some way have incriminated himself.

In short it is not a protective right if you actually use it to protect yourself and it is certainly not a right if you don't know about it. This is not only a strange piece of logic in itself but contrary to the normal legal assumption that ignorance of the law is no excuse. Knowledge of the law is simply assumed if you break it but not if you exercise your rights. The case went to the Court of Appeal where Lord Justice Lawton refuted the logic but also refuted any notion of a basic legal right to silence. Lord Diplock's notion that everyone had a right to remain silent without guilt being inferred was simply 'not in accord with the commonsense of ordinary folk'. Silence could mean guilt:

> The law has long accepted that an accused person is not bound to incriminate himself; but it does not follow that a failure to answer an accusation or question when an answer could reasonably be expected may not provide some evidence in support of an accusation. Whether it does will depend on the circumstances.

This rested on *R.* v. *Christie* (1914) which established that a person's reaction to an accusation against him could incriminate him if, by his conduct or demeanour, he seemed to accept the validity of the accusation. Scots law would seem from *Lewis* v. *Blair* (1858) to have traditionally taken the same line. When one accused person made a statement to a policeman on arrest, and the other stayed silent, the judge agreed it was relevant to propose an inference of guilt from the silence.

These cases refer to questioning by a policeman, but silence in the face of accusations by someone who is not 'in authority' is taken even more readily as indicative of guilt. In *Parkes* v. *The Queen* (1976) it was concluded that where a person is accused of something.

it is reasonable to expect that he or she will immediately deny it and that the absence of such a denial is some evidence of an admission on the part of the person charged and of the truth of the charge.

The basis for this is that the parties concerned are 'on even terms', as opposed to being an individual versus the power of the state in the guise of a policeman. But *R.* v. *Chandler* (1976) allowed the same reasoning in police-accused encounters so long as the accused was brought onto even terms by having his solicitor present. This is a nice example of a pattern that occurs repeatedly—adding protection for the accused with one hand and taking it away with the other, the factor introduced to try and add to the accused's protection becoming the very thing that legitimises reducing it.

How these rulings operate in court can be demonstrated by Case 103. The accused was found on the same floor of a multi-storey car park as a car which had been broken into and goods stolen. His car was on the same floor. Some of the stolen goods were on the ground beside the burgled car but others were not on him or found in the vicinity. The accused said another car had driven past him from that floor as he was approaching. Nonetheless he was incriminated by three things. First because he was there; second because he was looking at the stolen car with its boot open and the remaining contents on the ground beside it; third, and this was what the judge fixed on, because when the owners of the burgled car arrived and asked what he was doing he walked away towards his own car *without answering*.

He explained he just wanted nothing to do with it. The judge intervened.

Judge: It might be suggested that the obvious answer you'd make if you'd been doing nothing is 'nothing' [and here the well-spoken judge lapses into Glaswegian dialect] 'ah'm gaun fur ma caur'. Was that not to invite suspicion?

In cross-examination the prosecutor, again with the active involvement of the judge, made a big issue of this lack of response.

Prosecutor: Why did you not say—you were the only person in the world who knew—'a minivan just went down past me. Hurry, if we're quick we might get him'?

The accused tried to explain that he was anxious about being blamed and did not think so clearly, but the judge, who was taking what in effect was an active cross-examination role, interrupted.

Judge:       Look it's a simple question. Answer it.
Accused:     I didn't know that van had done it. [A point absolutely accurate in law.] It could have been done hours ago for all I knew.
Judge:       [angrily] Let me finish. Why did you not say . . . [repeating the point].

The accused replied he had not had time to think so clearly. The prosecutor took his turn:

Prosecutor:   Come, come, come, what kind of story is this you're trying to tell the ladies and gentlemen. You're frightened of being accused but you're so soft you don't blame anyone else, Mr McG.? . . . Why did you not say instead: 'Look, old chap, there's my insurance. There's my driving licence, I'm a window cleaner, look in the boot' like you did to the police? 'Leave me alone. You've caused enough trouble'?

The accused maintained he did not know who the real culprit was, it was not his business and in any case he panicked, he was shocked. The judge seized on this:

Judge:       You see if you got a shock it might be suggested that was all the more reason for saying it because you 'hadnae time to think aboot it.' It would just bubble out spontaneously.
Prosecutor:   But you were content to walk away.

The accused was found guilty and sentenced to nine months in prison. The accused's silence in the face of pre-caution questioning by the police—and even more readily by someone else—may be construed as evidence against him—only 'in certain circumstances' but since these circumstances are not specified in advance but assessed after the event this is not a right on which one securely bases a case.

Sometimes, the circumstances are specified to an extent indeed where they effectively mean the accused has to prove his innocence and can be presumed guilty if he does not answer police questions. In specified cases of suspected theft or receiving where the accused is found in possession of recently stolen goods and remains silent when accused, it is quite legal for the police to infer guilt from his silence and charge him and for the judge to instruct the jury they may infer this too (*Cryans* v. *Nixon*, 1955). But the accused is not warned of this. Indeed this is exactly how the gap between rhetoric and actual procedure may itself facilitate conviction. The generalised rights of justice—to be proved guilty, to remain silent, to see a solicitor—are not just the property of philosophers; they are publicly coined phrases. People may even believe they have these rights, to be used with impunity, and act upon them. So one gets examples like Case 91.

According to the doctrine of recent possession (shared by England and Scotland), when someone is found in possession of stolen goods, theft or receiving can be presumed without proof of the offence being committed unless the accused positively raises a reasonable doubt against it, so long as two additional conditions are met. First the goods must be recently stolen and second there must be other incriminating circumstances. In this case, the driver of a car stolen some weeks before in another part of the country was stopped by the police, a case of recent possession. The prosecutor produced as his other incriminating circumstances two points. First, the accused's attitude on being stopped was cool and collected, 'couldn't care less' according to police evidence, whereas the innocent citizen would, he suggested, be indignant. Second he refused to produce his log book or answer questions, and asked to see a solicitor. The defence of course refuted this interpretation. Remaining silent was not an incriminating circumstance but a constitutional right. His defence rested on

> . . . a matter fundamental to our law. . . . You may think when the evidence is over so quickly it is all clear. But something central is involved—the right of the individual to remain silent. . . . I do not suggest that a person who stands on his constitutional rights is necessarily innocent but I do suggest that where a person takes up his constitutional rights he is not to be criticised and it is not to be taken by you as an indication of guilt. . . .

The defence counsel argued on the grounds of the rhetoric of justice but the prosecutor won on the grounds of the law. For what the rhetoric overlooks is the statutory requirements of the 1968 Theft Act that it is up to the accused found in possession of goods that have been stolen to explain himself if he is not to be assumed guilty. So the prosecutor could point out 'He had every opportunity to clear the matter up and he failed to do so.' The judge, in his summing up, focused on the accused's reply that he would not answer until he had seen a solicitor and asked: 'Is this the remark of an innocent man?' (Case 91). Accepting the right against self-incrimination offered in the rhetoric of justice thus itself becomes an incriminating circumstance which allows for presumption of guilt.

But what about after the caution? After all it explicitly informs the accused that he need not answer charges or questions and indeed warns that statements may be used against him. It does not, however, warn that silence may also be used in evidence against him. Nor indeed would one expect it to in the same breath as telling him he has a right not to answer. And a whole line of cases like *Robertson* v. *Maxwell* (1951) in Scotland and *R.* v. *Naylor* in England make exactly this point:

> We do not think that the words of the caution can be properly construed in the sense that the prisoner remains silent after being cautioned at his peril and may find his silence made a strong point against him at his trial. (*R.* v. *Naylor* 1933)

Yet cases of this being allowed do occur, with the narrow subcategorisations of legal knowledge to legitimise them. According to Heydon's text on evidence (Heydon, 1975) a judge may always inform a jury that silence even after caution *strengthens* the prosecution case, though it does not *corroborate* it. A judge may invite the jury to take into account in the weight of the evidence that by not mentioning his story to the police, he has deprived them of the opportunity of investigating it (*R.* v. *Littleboy*, 1934). Lord Justice Stevenson, in *R.* v. *Ryan* (1966), distinguished the inference of guilt from allowing silence to affect credibility:

> It is we think clear. . . that it is wrong to say to a jury 'because the accused exercised what is undoubtedly his right, the privilege of remaining silent, you may draw an inference of guilt'; it is quite a different matter to say, 'this accused, as he is entitled to do, has

not advanced at an earlier stage the explanation that has been offered to you today; you, the jury, may take that into account when you are assessing the weight which you think it right to attach to that explanation.'

This distinction—and indeed that between corroboration and adding weight—may be philosophically accurate but the impact is the same. Indeed Lord Justice Salmon in *R.* v. *Sullivan* noted:

> The line dividing what may be said and what may not be said is a very fine one and it is perhaps doubtful whether in a case like the present it would be even perceptible to the members of an ordinary jury. (1967)

Indeed in the appeal on *Chandler* which began this discussion, Lord Justice Lawton's rebuke of the trial judge was not so much over the net result, inferring guilt, but over the style of reasoning used, to 'short circuit the intellectual process which had to be followed.' In short, such distinctions superficially uphold the rhetoric but boil down to little more protection than taking two logical steps instead of one. So judge and jury *may* infer guilt from the exercising of the right to silence; the accused *may* incriminate himself by exercising the privilege against self-incrimination.

But both statements and silence are of course only responses *as reported by the police*. They are unlikely to have been witnessed and they may never have happened. Even the fact that they are rarely challenged by the accused does not mean they actually happened. The defendant may not remember or may not think it worthwhile contradicting the police—there are after all always two police witnesses in Scotland to provide corroboration and in both systems that authoritative notebook—on something he cannot prove or indeed which may rebound on him if he happens to have a previous record.[12] Evidence of the accused's replies, confessions, silence, and demeanour therefore has to be set in context: neither the methods used to produce statements, nor indeed the validity of police reports, is subject to any effective controls.

## CONTROLS

There are four potential checks in the present legal structure, legal advice for the suspect, an independent witness at the police station, governmental directions, and judicial sanctions. The structure, substance, and practice of the law make them all too weak.

There is no systematic on-the-spot check in the police station on advice given, methods used, or the validity of statements read out in court, and without that there is no way of enforcing *at the time* the prohibition of 'bullying, pressure or third-degree methods' to secure answers to questions. It is hardly surprising then that cases of 'verballing' arise, like the infamous *Challenor* case[13] or that Cain should find policemen saying, for example: 'I must say I've never told a lie in court myself but I have often said things that were not quite the truth' (1971, p. 91).

Judges and official committees and inquiries have recognised that police malpractices or errors may occur in the privacy of the police station. The Fisher Report recognised this. Lord Devlin has observed:

> Statements have sometimes been put in evidence which have been said to be the prisoner's own unaided work as taken down by the police officer and with which the prisoner has recounted in the stately language of the police station (where, for example, people never eat but partake of refreshment and never quarrel but indulge in altercations) the tale of his misdeeds. (1960, p. 39)

Lord Cooper showed the same suspicions in the *Rigg* case (inauspiciously named, one cannot help feeling):

> I am bound to say that I have viewed with growing uneasiness and distaste the frequency with which in recent years there have been tendered in support of prosecutions alleged voluntary statements said to have been made to the police by persons charged then or subsequently, with grave crime. . . . To my mind, it is quite incredible that such a statement could have been taken from any person, least of all from a person of the age and apparent experience and condition of the accused, as a truly spontaneous and voluntary statement in the sense in which that expression has been used in the decision, or without such interrogation as would in common experience be indispensable to the taking of such a detailed precognition. (*H.M.Adv.* v. *Rigg*, 1946)

It is the sense of a need for some witnessing of what happens at the police station that has led both the Thomson Committee on Criminal Procedure in Scotland and the Criminal Law Revision Committee to recommend the use of tape-recorders (though not just to protect the accused but 'also to protect the police against unjustified allegations'—Thomson Committee, 1975 p. 38). This is one reason too why Fisher has recommended that there should be a clearer right to a solicitor at the police station and a public defender system to make this a real right for everyone, and why Thomson has proposed that in the post-charge situation an accused who wants to make a voluntary statement should be offered an interview with a solicitor. The other reason, of course, is to make legal advice obtainable to someone at the police station so that he knows what rights he has anyway.

But for the moment the accused is alone with the police and the formal structure creates an informal situation of unilateral power. The police are in the position to define what may be an ambiguous situation for the accused with no contradictory expertise to challenge it. Arrest, search, fingerprinting, questioning, being charged are all part of a degradation ritual which constructs an atmosphere of guilt. Alone with the police the accused is exposed to only one version of how the law defines his behaviour or alleged behaviour, how the evidence looks against him, be he innocent or guilty, and what his chances are in court. Given their own involvement, interests, and indeed beliefs in the case the police are likely to create, with the best will in the world, a sense of pending conviction which makes co-operation, not silence, the only sensible reaction. Indeed American police manuals, and English Police Review editorials (Release, 1973, p. 9) provide lists of techniques designed to produce precisely this effect. The first technique of interrogation listed in Inbau and Reid's manual is: 'Display an Air of Confidence in the Subject's Guilt' (1974 pp. ix).

Lord Justice General Cooper has noted:

> In the eyes of every ordinary citizen the venue [the police station] is a sinister one. When he stands alone in such a place confronted by several officers, usually some of high rank, the dice are loaded against him . . . (*Chalmers* v. *H.M.Adv.*, 1954)

Yet though this was the summing up in a full bench case with all the force of common law, he made no recommendation for some check to be introduced, not even the most obvious one of having a lawyer at hand.

This whole issue might seem a bit odd given that the 1887 Criminal Procedure (Scotland) Act laid down that prisoners should have access to 'a law agent' before and during any police examination:

> where any person has been arrested on any criminal charge, such person shall be entitled immediately upon arrest to have information sent to any properly qualified law agent that his professional assistance is required by such person, and informing him of the place to which such person is to be taken for examination; and such law agent shall be entitled to have a private interview with the person accused before he is examined on declaration and to be present at such examination . . . (s. 17)

Indeed it specified there should be forty-eight hours' delay if necessary to ensure the attendance of the lawyer.

The 1887 Act in short would appear to establish unequivocably the accused's statutory right to a solicitor on arrest and during questioning. But the judges have interpreted it differently. The abstract right has been qualified and the mechanics for putting it into operation have quite deliberately *not* been introduced. The judges have qualified the statutory right by refining the definition of the point at which it comes into play. The statute said 'on arrest' but the three-stage model of investigation blurs this. Being charged and being taken into custody were in 1887 the same thing: now there is the limbo of the uncharged suspect in custody but the accused's right to access to a solicitor is only when he is charged. This reasoning thus legitimises not only questioning in custody but questioning without access to, or the presence of, a solicitor. This was clearly established by 1926 when it was noted in the *Aitken* case as one of the disadvantages of the suspect *vis-à-vis* the charged prisoner.

What is more the judges have failed to control violations. In *Cheyne* v. *McGregor* (1941) the Lord Justice Clerk decided that, although it was 'altogether wrong' according to statute to refuse private consultation with a solicitor and that such consultation was 'a very important and valuable right—I should not object to it being described as a constitutional right', he was nonetheless:

> not prepared to assent to the view that in every case where a mistake is made, and the accused person is wrongly refused an

interview, the effect of that must be to bring the whole proceedings both at that time and forever to an end.

Violating the constitutional right need not therefore be sanctioned.
In England the Judges' rules demonstrate the knack of reiterating the rhetoric but qualifying it in a way that can negate it:

> . . . every person at any stage of an investigation should be able to communicate privately with a solicitor, *provided that in such a case no unreasonable delay or hindrance is caused to the process of investigation or the administration of justice by his doing so.* (Principle(c); my emphasis)

This is exactly the opposite of the provision of the Scottish 1887 Act whereby a delay in proceedings, far from constituting reasons for *not* calling a solicitor, was seen as a necessary measure to be instituted in order to ensure one was present. The police themselves decide whether 'unreasonable delay or hindrance' will be caused—that is to say, those who are supposed to be checked by the presence of a solicitor decide whether a solicitor should be present, an odd state of affairs to say the least. There is one check on them of course, the view of the High Court judges should the case be appealed. But they have elected to sit on the fence on this issue. The Court of Appeal has said it is 'unsatisfactory' to interpret 'delay or hindrance' as meaning simply that the accused might not confess with a solicitor there, but with the nice skill High Court judges have of both having their cake and eating it, they also refused to prohibit this or treat it as grounds for appeal, since it was a matter for the discretion of the trial judge (*R. v. Lemsatef*, 1977).

Duty solicitor schemes in Scotland and parts of England have to be set in this context. Studies[14] have indicated that the value of such schemes can be more symbolic than real, given not only police failure to encourage prisoners to contact solicitors, but also the reluctance of solicitors themselves to provide a twenty-four hour service. Generally they meet prisoners for the first time just before their first court appearance. But however the practices of police and solicitors might be 'reformed' the legal context would still impose a barrier. So far as interrogation before charge is concerned there is no clear right to a solicitor at all.

Nor is that a situation which has, as it were, crept in inadvertently or been overlooked by officialdom. Rather proposals to reform it have been rejected outright by Lord Widgery in England:'Any rule requiring the presence of the suspect's lawyer during interrogation is quite unacceptable' (Zander, 1972), and by the Thomson Committee (1975) in Scotland:

> We recommend that a solicitor should not be permitted to intervene in police investigations before charge. The purpose of the interrogation is to obtain from the suspect such information as he may possess regarding the offence, and this purpose might be defeated by the participation of his solicitor (p. 34)

—a statement that echoes the more direct objection by the police who do not want a solicitor at the police station because he would tell the accused to exercise his right to silence.

Judicial 'clarification' of the statutory right to a solicitor thus denies it at the time it is most needed and defines its value as a check on the interrogation of a suspect out of existence.

As to the mechanics of operating such right to a solicitor as there is, the police are under no obligation, contrary to the American ruling in *Miranda* v. *Arizona* (1966) to tell the accused of his rights. There is a contradiction in the 1887 Act to which the Scottish textbook, Renton and Brown (1972), draws attention. It 'imposes no duty upon anyone to inform the accused of his right to summon professional assistance but this should always be done.' (p. 3). It is not really a contradiction, of course, merely an omission to specify the mechanics to bring the right into operation—an omission which itself contributes to the gap between rhetoric and reality by offering symbolic rights but no instrumental access to them, just as the Factory Acts did (Carson, 1973). However it is an omission which case law could readily have tackled. But the judges have taken the opposite line. They have used the lack of specified enforcement mechanism in the Act to legitimise the police failure to inform the accused of any right to see a solicitor.

They do this by focusing on the word 'entitled' in the statutes and interpreting this as meaning entitled *if he asks* for a solicitor, *not* entitled to be told he may. He is not, in short, entitled to be told what he is entitled to. Again, by decontextualising the word from the apparent intention of the Act, the intention is nullified by judicial reasoning. Parliament is overruled by the judges, and the statute becomes a source for the general principles that constitute the rhetoric of justice, while the interpretation of case law becomes the very different legal reality.

How this operates in court may be demonstrated from observation.[15] The defence counsel was arguing that the accused had a right to a solicitor at the police station. The judge ruled that he was wrong—a suspect's right to be allowed to consult a solicitor did not of course mean that the policeman was under any obligation to tell the defendant of this: 'allowed means what it says'. The young barrister incidentally tried to get over this by telling the jury in his summing up that his argument was not just concocted by himself, someone who might be thought to be wet behind the ears but was the view expressed by someone who was definitely not wet behind the ears, Sir Henry Fisher, in his official report. However, the judge dismissed this. The view he said was not a statement of current law but a recommendation as to what it should be, and he added 'of no authority' anyway, being merely the opinion of an *ex*-High Court Judge! More important than judicial snideness, however, is the demonstration here of how structural contradictions influence the process and outcome of cases. The confidence of both counsel and judge that their interpretations were each correct though apparently contradictory is once again understandable if set in the context of the legal structure. The counsel's argument is based on statute and rhetoric, the judge's on the very different legal reality of case law. One cannot help but conclude from such examples of judicial interpretation of statutes that the ideology of the separation of powers leaving the judges free to protect the citizen from the government can be rendered somewhat ironical by what the judges do.

Indeed this point is supported further still. The Home Office has issued a circular (31 May 1966) instructing that attention should be drawn to a notice at the police station displaying the accused's rights. But the sanction, as we have seen, lies with the judges, and the judges have ruled that failure to do this 'is not necessarily fatal to the case'.

Finally there are ways in which a person who does wish to see a solicitor may be discouraged from—or punished for—doing so. The first is based on observation in court which suggests that asking for a solicitor may be treated as incriminating evidence. In Case 91, as already demonstrated, the accused's response, refusing to produce a log book or answer questions and requesting to see a solicitor was commented on by the judge to the jury:'Is this the remark of an innocent man?'

The second is more clearly a product of the legal structure as opposed to the interpretation of law by a lower court judge. It is financial. The Duty Solicitor scheme has been the norm in Scotland for some time but it is not general in England. Of course there is legal aid but Sir Henry Fisher notes limitations on the funding of legal advice at the police station with the implication that the accused would have to pay legal costs himself if the police drop the charge, and that the police are more likely to drop the charge if a solicitor is present—a vicious circle with the accused losing out either in freedom or finance.

The law thus explicitly prohibits at some stages, implicitly denies or discourages at others, access to a solicitor. Zander (1972) has shown that 74 per cent of a sample who asked to see a solicitor at the police station were refused, while Baldwin and McConville found that 70 per cent of defendants did not ask to see a solicitor while being interrogated and of those who did six out of seven were told they were not allowed to (1977, p.105). Given the legal context this is hardly surprising.

Enforcement is thus left to the *post hoc* decisions of the courts. And so for that matter are the rules to be enforced. Certainly there is a code of government directions for police conduct with suspects, the Judges' rules, drawn up by High Court Judges and issued by the Home Office to the police. Their impact may be suggested by Sir Henry Fisher's finding in his inquiry into the *Confait* case that some policemen did not know, understand or at any rate obey the rules. He therefore recommends better publicity. What is more important, however, is that whether they are known or not, abided by or broken, there is no machinery to enforce them, *not even* the judicial sanction of exclusion of evidence in court—inadmissibility.

Inadmissibility is the major weapon available to the court to control police practices. The Judges' Rules are the most explicit statement of controls on police practices. But the rules and the machinery for punishment do not cohere. Breach of the Judges' Rules does not automatically lead to inadmissibility. Indeed according to *R. v. Prager* (1972) it is not even clear that a judge is *allowed*, at his discretion, to exclude information that has been obtained by methods that breach the rules unless it is also proved to have been involuntarily given.

There is a simple enough reason for this. The Judges' Rules are not law, just administrative directions, and not enforceable in court. As Lord Devlin (1960) puts it:

It must never be forgotten that the Judges' Rules were made for the guidance of the police and not for the circumscription of the judicial power. (p. 39)

Indeed it has been held in the *Prager* case that a voluntary confession made in breach of the rules could not be made inadmissible exactly because that 'would exalt the Judges' Rules into rules of law'. So while the Judges' Rules are often referred to in court, while they are judge-made and in part based on common law, and while they may give rise to questions of inadmissibility, they are of themselves rules without teeth.

The underlying cause of this situation interestingly enough is the democratic ideology of the separation of powers, whereby judges shall not be the lackeys of the government, in order to prevent political manipulation and protect the civil liberties of the citizen against the state—interestingly, because it is precisely protection of civil liberties that the Judges' Rules might claim to be providing. So a state structure geared to the dominant ideology of democratic rights prevents specific rulings to preserve those democratic rights from being enforced. The structure behind democratic ideology thus ironically legitimises the failure to enforce it.

We must therefore look to judicial sanctions in the courts for control on the collection and presentation of evidence. Judicial sanctions rest on the notion of inadmissibility, on the judge's right to exclude evidence obtained by illegal means. Police conduct in collecting evidence is controlled by the possibility of losing their case if their conduct does not meet legal standards. This *means* of control severely limits its value as a control.

First it can by its nature affect only those cases actually brought to trial (or indeed to appeal) and of course the vast majority of defendants plead guilty, partly because of what happens in their encounter with the police, while the structural barriers to appeals are such that few are allowed. As a control over routine police behaviour in *all* cases, whether they actually end up being brought to trial or not, this method is really a non-starter. What is more, it depends on a case being made out by the defendant on the methods used, and there we are back to square one: no witnesses at the police station, the problems of proof and credibility, a trial in itself involved in raising the issue for control. Indeed when such questions arise in trial by jury, the jury is sent away and 'a trial within a trial' is held to decide how to continue. The police are therefore controlled only by the defendant successfully making a case against them in the course of his own trial.

Second, since inadmissibility involves a *post hoc* decision, the rules themselves are never clear until they are tested in the courts after the event. Indeed it was the police themselves, after two contradictory decisions by judges on the legitimacy of their conduct, who asked for the first Judges' Rules in 1912. Since the rules are still subject to common law decisions, however, the situation has altered little in practice. If rules that lack enforcement make feeble controls, rules that are not known till after they have been broken are feebler still.[16]

Third, inadmissibility is not an absolute control. Even where the conduct of the police is declared illegitimate by the judges, the evidence acquired by that conduct is not necessarily excluded, and the case can still be won by the prosecution regardless. There is no equivalent in Scots or English law of the American doctrine that the fruit of the forbidden tree is itself forbidden—inadmissible (*Mapp* v. *Ohio* 1961). Scots law on exclusion of evidence is sometimes described as clearer and fairer to the accused, much more geared to disciplining the police via the power of exclusion than English law. Heydon (1975, p. 230) suggests this citing Lord Justice General Cooper's exclusion of unwarranted search evidence in *Lawrie* v. *Muir* in support. But the same judge regularly admitted illegally obtained evidence, for example, because it was taken 'in good faith' (*Fairley* v. *Fishmongers of London*, 1951), although he had ruled out good faith as a good reason just the year before. Indeed Lord Justice General Cooper had made it clear that the evidence he declared inadmissible in *Lawrie* v. *Muir* was defined as such mainly because it was *not* the police who obtained it:

> It is especially to be noted that the two inspectors who in this instance exceeded their authority were not police officers *enjoying a large residuum of common law discretionary powers*, but the employees of a limited company acting in association with the Milk Marketing Board, whose only powers are derived from contracts between the Board and certain milk producers and distributors, of whom the appellant is not one. Though the matter is narrow, I am inclined to regard this last point as sufficient to tilt the balance against the prosecution. (1950; my emphasis)

This is hardly a raising of the standards of civil rights against illegal *police* activity. However, the image of Scots law as fair and operating tight controls on the police, may be understandable if it is compared with the extremes in English law. In *Kuruma* v. *R.*, a 1955 case of illegally obtained evidence (the evidence itself being rather dubious anyway), English judges went so far as to justify their decision by citing a judicial opinion of 1861 that effectively declared anything goes: 'It matters not how you get it; if you steal it even it would be admissible.' Ducking the inadmissibility issue means that even the principle of *post hoc* control of police behaviour via the courts' power to exclude evidence is avoided.

Fourth, as this chapter and indeed this whole study demonstrates, the line drawn between the admissible and the inadmissible by the judges in exercising control over the police has been far from rigid. But in drawing that line they are not just exercising control in a specific case, they are also making the rules for the future. The judges have not chosen to use their powers to exclude evidence to offer clear-cut protection of the accused's alleged rights. Rather, with every questionable practice that is admitted and so legitimised, case law has whittled these 'rights' away.

# 4 Pleading Guilty[1]

Given the extent of legal police powers to acquire and construct incriminating evidence, and the broad scope for admitting it as evidence in court, it may be hardly surprising that most defendants never force the prosecutor to prove his case at a trial but incriminate themselves in the most direct way by pleading guilty. Sample studies show that 76 to 93 per cent of defendants in Magistrates' courts and 57 to 75 per cent in higher courts plead guilty, (Dell, 1971; Zander, 1969; Bottoms and McClean, 1976; Baldwin and McConville, 1977). This proportion includes not only those who see themselves as factually guilty, or factually innocent but technically guilty (both of whom according to the rhetoric still have a right to force the prosecution to prove guilt), but those who see themselves as completely innocent. The encounter with the police, be it the definitional encounter in petty offences against public order, or the more complicated process of arrest, interrogation, or search in 'real crime', is the essence of criminal justice for most of the people who turn up for their ritual plea and sentence in court. Indeed the very nature of most courtroom appearances as routine, boring, ritual, unproblematic processing, as described by Carlen (1976), or Bottoms and McClean makes particular sense in the context of what has gone before—the matter is already effectively decided. Baldwin and McConville's recognition that the lack of safeguards for the accused in custody can lead to forced—or fabricated—statements and a plea of guilty touches just the tip of the iceberg. The whole gamut of pre-trial procedures contributes to the same sense of the defence case as a lost cause long before the trial, either by the defendant himself or by defence counsel,[2] and the defendant ends up pleading guilty.

Most studies of the guilty plea have focused not so much on the legal context surrounding either the preliminaries to the plea or the plea itself, but on the interactional, informal, and bureaucratic aspects of plea bargaining (Newman, 1966; Blumberg, 1967; Skolnick, 1967; Baldwin and McConville, 1977). Alliances (often frowned on as unholy) and negotiations between prosecutor and defence counsel or indeed between counsel and judge are focused on as the mechanism; the bureaucratic need for a speedy and efficient throughput of cases is focused on as the motivation. Bottoms and McClean (1976) conclude from their observations that court workloads are such that 'the smooth administration of justice essentially depends on the co-operation of the mass of defendants' (p. 6)—the co-operation of pleading guilty. So we are presented with a picture where the legal system is geared to notions like: everyone has the right to a fair trial, the burden of proof is on the prosecutor, no-one is bound to incriminate himself—but in the course of doing their job the administrators of justice undermine this system for the sake of efficiency and the net result is all sorts of pressures to plead guilty. There are two dangers in this 'law in action' perspective. First, approaching the guilty plea via administrative pressures paints too neutral a picture of the criminal process—bureaucracy is a neutral word: what it is *for* is important. Second it overplays non-legal motivations at the expense of the part played by the legal system itself.

## NEUTRAL BUREAUCRATS?

The emphasis on administrative needs—epitomised in Bottoms and McClean's 'liberal bureaucrat'—presents a picture of neutral officials whose sole aim is efficiency and for whom conviction is merely a by-product. This is not necessarily the case. It would after all be even speedier at the legislative level to decriminalise general categories of behaviour, especially given the triviality of most cases that come before the courts, and the magistrates' courts in particular, or at the administrative level, to drop specific cases. This is within the discretion of police and prosecution and indeed it is defined in the Scots manual as the duty of the procurator fiscal to decide, among other things, 'whether the act or omission charged is of sufficient importance' and 'whether there is sufficient evidence in support of these facts to justify the institution of criminal proceedings' (Renton and Brown, 1972, p. 19). Of course cases are dropped where there is not enough legal proof for prosecution. Indeed Mack (1976) points out that big-time criminals know exactly how to manage the system in order to ensure there will not be enough proof. But where there is some hope that the accused will plead guilty, the case will not necessarily be dropped, even where it is known that it could not stand up in court. Thus police complaint files come back from the procurator fiscal with notes in the margin like this: 'If not guilty, desert, can't identify.' The accused pleaded not guilty and the case, after four adjournments, was dropped. Other cases work out differently. In a case annotated thus: 'If not guilty, reconsider, doubt if it can be proved', the accused, who had been stopped while taking copper piping worth a pound from a lorry to a broker, and accused of stealing it, pleaded guilty and was duly sentenced. Prosecutions thus continue even when the prosecutor knows from the evidence that the accused is either in real or in legal terms not guilty. He does not necessarily drop cases for which he could not meet the burden of proof in court; he simply hopes he will not have to.

These were only two cases out of 100 randomly selected police complaint files. But Baldwin and McConville would seem to offer supporting evidence for prosecution cases that could not in fact be proved succeeding because of a guilty plea. Independent assessors concluded that acquittal would have been possible or likely in 21 per cent of the 121 cases in their sample because the prosecution evidence was weak (1977, p. 74). But although many of these defendants claimed innocence on interview, all of them had pleaded guilty and the prosecutor never had to prove his case. The rhetoric of the burden of proof therefore did nothing to protect them.

What these examples suggest is that administrative pressures for speed and efficiency should not be taken as some neutral influence with the incidental product of a high conviction rate without a lot more research into the motivations behind dropping or pursuing cases. It is not without significance that Bottoms and McClean cite and sympathise with the administrative problems and motivations of their 'liberal bureaucrats' without any empirical scrutiny at all to check out either their problems or their motivation. The image of the overworked court has become a cliché that can be referred to without further analysis. But are the courts overworked? What level of work constitutes overwork? On routine visits to the courts one can certainly come across afternoon sessions that begin at 2 p.m. and finish at twelve minutes past. In any case Laurence Friedmann's (1978) historical study demonstrates that Alamena County Courts in the late nineteenth century, though *not* crowded urban courts, still operated routinely by plea-bargaining. The four adjournments noted in the case above where the prosecution could not be sure of conviction suggest that some lengths were gone to, to strengthen the case before giving it up—in short, that efficiency was defined not so much in terms of securing a speedy throughput of cases as in terms of securing convictions. Administrative motivation may be less value-free than is normally suggested.

More important, the emphasis on bureaucratic and other non-legal influences distracts from the role of the legal system itself in pressurising people to plead guilty. For if all sorts of interests which may have nothing to do with the law *per se* provide the motives for plea-bargaining it is the legal system itself which provides the opportunity.

## LEGAL STRUCTURE AND GUILTY PLEA

Discussions of plea-bargaining in England have drawn attention to the differences in English and American prosecution structures, and concluded that the general structure of prosecution in England does not create so much of an opportunity for putting pressures on the defendant to plead guilty. Nor is it seen to be a practice with official endorsement. Rather it is, as Carlen (1976) puts it, something to be hidden from the magistrate, 'a betrayal of the professional construction of justice' (p. 35). But one cannot conclude from the differences between American and English legal structures, and the covert nature of plea-bargaining in England, that it is not structurally or authoritatively promoted. Philip Thomas (1978) makes the point that although overt judicial plea-bargaining is frowned on in case law, structural factors allowing *covert* judicial plea-bargaining are established by it—an example of how case law can both uphold and deny the rhetoric of justice. Cases allow counsel to give his client 'advice in strong terms' as to his plea (*R. v Turner*, 1970), and allows counsel and judge to meet privately and discuss the case and potential sentence (*R. v. Turner*, 1970; *R. v. Cain*, 1976). What is not allowed is the barrister actually telling the defendant that the advice he is giving emanates from discussion with the judge. Lord Widgery put it in a nutshell:

> One of the advantages that flowed from the close relationship between judge and barrister was that the barrister in that situation could go to the judge and ask him for guidance. If the judge felt disposed to give it to him, counsel would then have a

reliable idea of what sort of sentence his client faced, and could advise him properly. But the whole point would be destroyed if he disclosed what the judge had told him. The confidentiality in their relationship would be broken. (*R. v. Peace*, 1975)

We are back[3] to one-step linkages being disapproved while two-step linkages to the same end are deemed quite legitimate.

In Scotland 'plea-adjustment' is not only facilitated by the structure of prosecution but is officially encouraged. The charge, the allocation of a case to solemn or summary jurisdiction (with higher or lower maximum sentences) and the acceptance of the plea are left, with the occasional statutory exception, to the prosecutor's discretion, and can be changed without explanation. There are clear parallels with Skolnick's study of the public prosecutor's role in America (1967) which he suggests creates the opportunity for bargaining. It is also officially endorsed, for example, by the Thomson Committee (1975):

> There is no statutory authority for plea adjustment but it is accepted as proper practice for either the accused's legal adviser or the prosecutor to approach the other and negotiate the acceptance of a partial plea. Normally such an approach comes from the defence but it is perfectly proper for the prosecutor to intimate to the defence that he would be willing to accept a plea of guilty to less than the full extent of any particular charge (p. 97)

The only criticism by the Committee was that it was wasteful for plea-bargaining to occur at the last minute after the case had been prepared and witnesses called, so it was proposed that: 'While the practice of plea adjustment should continue, it should wherever possible be effected well before the trial' (p. 97), and that procedures should be used or adapted for this purpose. The period of time between the charge and the plea diet should be extended from six to twenty days (too bad for those in custody untried) to 'facilitate early plea adjustment in solemn proceedings', and there should be a preliminary meeting between the two sides, at which:

> *We recommend that there should be informal discussion* between prosecution and defence . . . on, for example, the following subjects . . . plea adjustment . . . (p. 116; my emphasis).

In short, far from being some under-the-carpet subversion of official policy, plea-bargaining in Scotland has been recognised, endorsed, and promoted by an official committee.

But the legal system both in England and Scotland also pressurises defendants into pleading guilty, whether they consider themselves guilty or not, in more specific ways. There is for example a discount in sentence for pleading guilty—a clear and explicit example of how legal rules emasculate legal rhetoric. It may be a 'golden thread' of justice that the defendant has the right to make the prosecution prove his guilt, but should he exercise that right and be found guilty he will be given a heavier sentence. Not that the law phrases it like this; rather it is put in terms of a mitigated sentence for showing repentance by pleading guilty. But the effect is the same and this justification only demonstrates the reasoning by which the gap between rhetoric and law is maintained. We have already seen that, although self-incriminating statements made to the police are inadmissible if they are obtained by fear or inducement, sentencing policy is based precisely on inducement for the most self-incriminating statement of all—a guilty plea. There are other inducements too. In Scotland there is a special form to apply for an 'accelerated diet', in other words, quick disposal, if you plead guilty, an attractive proposition, especially for the defendant in custody losing wages and perhaps his job, and especially if he thinks he might as well plead guilty since, as some of the defendants interviewed put it:

You don't have a chance anyway.

People like us can't go against the police.

A copper's word would go against you if he came and lifted a bloke off the street.

I was surprised to hear them actually lie in the court but they can say anything and get away with it.

People like us don't have rights.

For the defendant with previous convictions there are particular pressures to plead guilty, particularly in England. Baldwin and McConville discuss the situation of the defendant with a record who wishes to defend himself by saying that the police statements are simply not true. They suggest that the tendency of defence counsel to advise a guilty plea instead is not soundly based in law, and cite the statement in R. v. *Thomas and Whittle* (1967) that: 'the appropriate sentence cannot be increased by an attack that may be made on the credibility of any witness' and suggest that the counsel's advice runs against this: 'This, however, is not a view apparently shared by some barristers' (1977, p. 47).

But the barrister's advice is not entirely misplaced. It may not be legal for attacks on the credibility of prosecution witnesses to affect the *sentence*, but it is perfectly legal for it to affect the evidence that can be introduced against the accused and so affect the *verdict*. The barrister quoted as mis-stating the law is absolutely right when he says: 'All this mud that you want to sling at the prosecution and the police, it's all going to come back on you.' According to the 1898 Criminal Evidence Act (s.1(f)(ii))whenever a defence case involves imputations against the character of a prosecution witness, the accused's bad character can be put before the court too. This has been interpreted in English law (though not in Scotland[4]) as involving any suggestion by the accused that prosecution witnesses are lying. If he does this the prosecutor can bring in as evidence the fact that the accused has previous convictions, a factor which the jury is not normally allowed to hear on the grounds that they might be tempted to convict on issues that have no bearing on the case in question. Having previously committed a crime is no evidence that he committed this one. But that rule goes by the board if the accused challenges the police or other prosecution witnesses. There is some discretion for the court to decide where the line is to be drawn, and there is some indication of a matter of degree involved in exactly what amounts to a challenge on character. So:

> It was one thing for the appellant to deny that he had made the confession: but it was another thing to say the whole thing was an elaborate and deliberate concoction on the part of the inspector. (*R.* v. *Jones*, 1923).

However, even if the accused does not make such a challenge on his own initiative it may be made for him and still count against him. In *R.* v. *Tanner* (1977) it was deemed quite legitimate for the defendant to be cross-examined on his previous record after his denial of police statements was interpreted for him by the judge into an attack on police character:

Judge:          It follows from that, does it not, Tanner, that the
                whole of the evidence of these two officers where

they say you admitted the offence, is made up?

Defendant:     Yes.

Prosecution counsel for their part have techniques for inducing the defendant himself to transform his own innocuous words into a form that will count legally as an attack on character:

Prosecutor:     And you say this before us is not the proceeds of shoplifting?

Defendant:     No, not that stuff, no.

Prosecutor:     And the police have invented this case against you, it must follow, mustn't it?

Defendant:     Well, I suppose so.

Prosecutor:     Well it's the only thing possible isn't it?

Defendant:     Yes . . .

Prosecutor:     You think they created this whole case against you?

Defendant:     *I am not calling them* liars but that's what happened. [My emphasis]

Prosecutor:     It's not good enough to say you are not calling them liars, because that is the only possibility if you are telling the truth.

Defendant:     Yes.[5]

This method of introducing damaging evidence against the defendant is all too easy. It is after all in the nature of the adversary system that the two sides offer conflicting versions of what occurred, each implying the other wrong: the scene is already set for negotiating an implicit into an explicit (and sanctioned) accusation.

In any case the court's discretion to decide where the line is to be drawn has had clear qualifications imposed by the House of Lords. In *Selvey* v. *D.P.P.*(1970) they agreed that the court might have some discretion to stop the prosecutor cross-examining the accused about his previous convictions, but they refused to agree that the discretion should be exercised in favour of the accused, even if it did put the accused in the double bind of being unable to develop a quite legitimate defence without giving the prosecutor a free hand to introduce unfavourable character evidence against him.

It may now be clear why Baldwin and McConville found 'those with prior criminal records were singled out as being vulnerable in these circumstances' to counsel's advice to plead guilty. In the current state of English law, counsel's advice to the defendant with a record to plead guilty rather than attack police 'verbals' for fear of mud slung at the police rebounding on him and a higher sentence resulting, is not so much misleading the defendant as summing up for him only too accurately his legal position. Attacking police evidence leaves him wide open to having his previous convictions made known in court and reducing his chances of a successful defence; pleading not guilty and failing means a heavier sentence.

Once a guilty plea is made the defendant tends to be stuck with it, since there are also structural obstacles in Scots law to altering a preliminary guilty plea to not guilty which do not exist in the reverse situation. 'The Crown is master of the instance', as Thomson puts it, so the prosecutor can accept the change to a guilty plea any time he chooses without explanation. But in the High Court and summary courts a change of plea to *not* guilty is only allowed at the discretion of the court if an adequate case is made out by the accused:

> it being necessary for him to satisfy the court that his plea was tendered under substantial error or misconception or in circumstances which tended to prejudice his case. (Renton and Brown, 1972, p. 95)

In jury cases in the sheriff court there is no statutory provision for withdrawing a guilty plea at all: it is legally impossible to change one's plea to not guilty. The Thomson Committee recommended that this should be made possible but only at the discretion of the court, not as of right.

Nor is there any attempt by the court, once a guilty plea is made, to check whether it is appropriate. It is simply accepted in court without examination of the circumstances or intent, though both may affect the legal applicability of the charge, and the validity of the prosecution case. A not guilty plea stands to be disproved; a guilty plea does not.

In all these ways then the pressures to plead guilty lie not just in negotiations, informal liaisons and bureaucratic interests, but also in the legal system itself. Criminal justice in principle places the onus of proof on the prosecution and provides the accused with the right to a trial and a presumption of innocence. But it operates in practice on the assumption that for the vast majority these rights must be merely empty rhetoric. As one prosecutor put it when asked about expanding legal aid: 'Good heavens we couldn't do that. They'd all want trials then.' The procedural devices built into the legal system ensure that the vast majority do not.

# 5 Strong and Weak Cases: the Trial in Context

The trial is the focal point of the ideology of democratic justice. Though the trial *per se* is older than democracy it assumed a form with the emergence of the democratic state which expressed a historically specific ideology of justice. Its emphasis on proof by a reasoned case reflected the victory of eighteenth-century 'rationality' over the superstition of trial by ordeal. Established rules of evidence and procedure date largely from the same period, expressing the end of arbitrariness and the establishment of the rule of law. The banner of Magna Carta and trial by jury was raised by Coke in the battle against absolute monarchy under the guise of resurrected tradition but also expressing the modern ideology of control by 'the people', as indeed did the demand that the trial must be public. The double-sided idea that the accused is presumed innocent till proved guilty and that the burden of proof lies with the prosecutor indicated a new ideological relationship between the citizen and the state: the citizen's liberty would be the norm and any interference or punishment by the state a matter for clear and public justification. This last double-sided idea is indeed depicted as the lynchpin of the ideology of justice.

Every law student must know the quotation from *Woolmington* v. *D.P.P.* (1935) on the burden of proof:

> Throughout the web of the English Criminal Law one golden thread is always to be seen, that it is the duty of the prosecution to prove the prisoner's guilt. . . .

Lord Devlin makes an impassioned plea for the right to silence as a consequence of the doctrine of the burden of proof:

> I hope that the day will never come when that right is denied to any Englishman. It is not a refuge of technicality; the law on this

matter reflects the natural thought of England. So great is our horror at the idea that a man may be questioned, forced to speak and perhaps condemn himself out of his own mouth that we afford to everyone suspected or accused of a crime, at every stage, and to the very end, the right to say: 'Ask me no questions, I shall answer none. Prove your case'. (*R.* v. *Adams*, 1957; Heydon, 1975, p. 151)

Scots law puts it more prosaically but just as strongly: 'It is a sacred and inviolable right that no man is bound to incriminate himself' (*Livingstone* v. *Murrays*, 1830).

The trial is the focal point of justice in another sense. It is the only part of the legal process which is open to the public and the press. This not only carries the potential for more control over what takes place, than for example, the secrecy of the police station; it also invests the trial with a particular ideological significance. It is the showcase of justice, the only place where a sample, whether representative or not, of the legal process is put on display. The High Court trial is also a showcase for the democratic state, for this is one point where the doctrine of the separation of powers is put on display and the *executive*, in the shape of the police, must hand over control to the avowedly neutral and independent judge. It is, in addition, the only stage at which an *élite* of the state is put on public view—not the amateur magistrates of the committal proceedings, the petty executives of the police or the court bureaucracy but the robed, wigged, aloof dignatories of the judiciary. If the ideology of justice is to have any credibility—and E. P. Thompson (1975) suggests an ideology cannot survive unless it is also seen to be effective (p. 263)—it is at this stage that one would expect it to be visibly in operation. The legal adage might aptly be reversed: what is *seen* to be done must pass as justice; the state's *public* practice must fit plausibly with its ideology. So, if it is a crucial demand of the ideology of justice that the prosecutor bears the burden of proof beyond reasonable doubt, one might well expect that he will indeed have to demonstrate this ideology in practice, before he can win his case. And in most cases[1] he must. In that sense justice may well be seen to be done.

What is *seen*, however, is but the proverbial tip of the iceberg. The trial is not an isolated event; it is part of a long process which takes place out of the public eye. Chapter 4 has shown how pressures which the public do *not* see mean that the vast majority of accused people do *not* make the prosecution prove guilt but incriminate themselves with a guilty plea. The trial is not just part of a larger process though; it is also the product of that process. What is *seen* in court is moulded by all sorts of unseen factors and what is not put on public display is exactly *how* the public version has been shaped, tailored, *and distorted* behind the scenes. If judge, jury, press, or public leave the court satisfied that the prosecutor has fulfilled his duty by making his case, that his case was clearly the stronger and that they have seen the ideology of justice in operation, they may be absolutely right—*in the light of what they have observed and heard.* What they have *not* seen and heard, however, might make them think again.

It has been argued that pre-trial filtering of cases is exactly why prosecutors tend to win in court, since the filtering is essentially a filtering out of weak prosecution cases leaving only the strong cases where the accused is almost incontrovertibly guilty to come to court at all. Remember Sir Robert Mark's comment, albeit less in explanation of why prosecutors win than in moral indignation that they should sometimes lose:

> The procedural safeguards for the suspect or accused in our system of criminal justice are such that committal for trial, involving the participation of lawyers and bench, is itself an indication of strong probability of guilt. (Alderson, 1973, p. 16)

But pre-trial procedures are not just about safeguards for the accused; they are also about conferring powers and imposing limitations on how each side can set about preparing its case for trial. Procedures do not then just filter out weak cases and filter in strong cases; they play a part in determining exactly how strong or weak a case can be.

They do so both at the general level of the relationship of prosecution and defence in an adversarial and accusatorial system, and at the specific level of the powers and limitations awarded each side by particular rulings of legal procedure. And they do so in a way which makes it likely that the prosecution case that comes to trial will be stronger than the accused's. The defence is placed at a disadvantage in three broad ways: in knowing the issues of the case, in access to evidence for his case, and in the ability to ensure witnesses are available to state his case, both in the sense of getting

them along to state their evidence in court at all and in having the
right to use the controls of contempt of court, prevarication or
perjury to make sure they do.


## KNOWING THE ISSUES

In a sense the accused really need not know much of the case against
him at all. Since the onus of proof is on the prosecution the defence
need not present a case at all, but simply pick holes in the
prosecution case to raise a reasonable doubt in the minds of those
judging him, or indeed say nothing at all. It may even be decided
after the prosecutor has put his case that there is 'no case to answer'.
But if the prosecutor does assemble a legally sufficient and logically
plausible case—and he is unlikely to take it as far as trial if it does not
appear to meet minimal standards—the accused really has to
present a positive alternative if he is to enter the battle for credibility
at all. Given this task, the defence is ironically enough in a weaker
position than the prosecution in building up a case exactly because
he is responding to a charge, not instigating it. The framework of
relevant issues (in both common-sense and legal terms) is set up by
the charge, and the defence has to be constructed within this
framework. Historically this fact was actually used to channel out
possible defences: 'An ingenious prosecutor could render any
defence inadmissible by explicitly contradicting it in the
indictment' (Gordon, 1968, p. 29).This particular technique is no
longer possible since the introduction of the shortened charge in
1887, but the Crown's prerogative in creating a framework of
relevance for information remains.

   Given the accused's position as respondent, it is obviously
essential that he should know exactly what the charge against him
is, and this is a procedural requirement in line with the doctrine of
'no surprise': 'It is improper for the counsel for the prosecution to
attempt to take the defence by surprise' (Arguile, 1969, p. 149). Of
course that does not mean much if the accused does not understand
the charge and, having received evidence that the esoteric language
of the charge may mystify rather than inform the accused, that
indeed people were pleading guilty without knowing what they
were accused of (p. 84), the Thomson Committee recommended
that the form of the charge should be simplified. This seems a step
towards the practical realisation of the accused's right in the

rhetoric of justice to know what he stands accused of. But there are limits to its value. For example the Scottish prosecutor fiscal also has a procedural power to alter the charge before the trial, while in England the reasons given for arrest need not be 'the charge which may ultimately be found in the indictment' (*Christie* v. *Leachinsky*, 1947). So it is that defendants complain that they are charged with one offence at the police station, come prepared to dispute that, only to find the charge has changed form:

> This is ridiculous. We want to complain about this. We were charged with resisting arrest then when we get to the court it's breach of the peace. (Case 17)

The problem was acknowledged but sustained by the Thomson Committee (1975):

> An arrestee must be told why he is arrested. As however it is the procurator fiscal who prepares the indictment or complaint which contains the charge against the accused in court, it follows that the charge made by the police may be different from the charge eventually libelled against the accused in court. . . . We do not see how this could be changed. (p. 24)

Nor does the doctrine of 'no surprise' stretch to the accused being informed of the *case* against him, though this can significantly affect his ability to prepare a case in response.

In England there are, for indictments at least, committal proceedings where the basis of the prosecution's case is publicly stated. This is designed not only to inform the accused of the case against him but for the bureaucratic purpose of deciding whether the case is strong enough to spend time and money taking it to trial, but it does also have the effect of putting the 'no surprise' doctrine into practice for the accused to some extent. The effect is limited since the prosecutor has no duty to call at the committal proceedings all the witnesses he intends to use at the trial (*R.* v. *Epping and Harlow J. J.*), and the defendant can be refused copies of additional evidence for the prosecution raised after committal proceedings. In Scotland, however, there is no public rehearsal of the prosecution case at all since the decision to prosecute is a matter for the private discretion of the prosecutor himself.

The Thomson Committee did recommend a revival of the old

judicial examination between charge and trial but that would not be in order to let the accused know the case against him. Indeed it would be for exactly the opposite purpose. It would not be the prosecutor but the accused who would have to present his version of an incident to the court and the purpose would be to put the 'no surprise' doctrine into practice for the prosecutor's advantage only, and explicitly take advantage of 'surprise' so far as the accused was concerned by forcing him to put his version on record *before* knowing the details of the case against him:

> In our opinion the best opportunity of obtaining the truth from the accused is immediately after he has been charged when he does not know the evidence against him. (Thomson, 1975, p. 188)

This would prevent him from producing alibis later or being:

> in a position to adjust his own evidence to meet the case against him. (Thomson, 1975, p. 188)

What is not even considered is that the prosecution might also have a case that can be 'adjusted' to meet the recorded version of the accused, recorded before he knows the context in which his own words can be used to incriminate him (for context does affect meaning), and recorded so that he cannot deviate from them later when he does know the context without losing credibility anyway. This of course is the precise purpose of the proposal and it is only the defendant, not the prosecutor, who is so constrained.

As so often in the Thomson Report the problem of ascertaining truth is defined purely in terms of the possibility of the accused 'fabricating' a case, not in terms of *both* cases being part of an artificial reconstruction process susceptible to 'adjustment' and distortion after the event.

But for the moment there are in Scotland no courtroom rehearsals of either case. The procedure is simply that the prosecutor gives the accused a list of his witnesses and vice-versa. (Even this is compulsory only in jury trials, not in the summary cases which constitute the vast majority of proceedings.) Only the names of the witnesses are provided, not the statements the prosecutor has put together from his witnesses. Though each side can interview the other party's witnesses it does not follow that this will reveal the points that the adversary is using to build up his jigsaw of a case. A witness for one side will not necessarily be freely co-operative with the other, so that the questioner only gets answers to the questions asked and without knowing the crux of the other's case he may not ask the right questions. Even the interpretation of the answers given may vary so that the final gloss on the statement for the Crown and the defence may be quite different. A defence lawyer is not entitled to see any statement attributed to the accused even though it may be read out in court as evidence against his client, and may be damaging to his case. In the first requirement for collecting evidence—knowing the relevant issues of the case—the prosecutor has the double advantage of not only defining the issues, but of being under no duty to disclose them till the trial.

## COLLECTING EVIDENCE

In the actual collection of evidence the advantage also lies with the Crown: the prosecutor is more likely to come across a breadth of potential evidence because of his superior facilities. Almost all prosecutions in Britain are presented by the state, not by an individual. This is even more clear-cut in Scotland than in England, where the police, even if only in legal fiction, prosecute as private citizens. Under Scots Law, the police do not conduct their own prosecutions but hand their cases over to procurators fiscal, legally trained and experienced civil servants under the aegis of the Lord Advocate. Prosecution is thus conducted by a professional public prosecutor who works full-time in court, for whom the establishment of a case in law and fact is a matter of routine, to whom the judges and clerks are colleagues, whose evidence is collected by a team of professional detectives, the police. The facilities for constructing the prosecution case are a publicly funded part of the legal structure, but defence is left to the private citizen and private enterprise.

This produces inequality between one accused and another according to class, since the accused has to buy the case he can afford. Legal advice, representation in court, the search for witnesses, the taking of statements, all have a price attached. It is market forces, tempered at the margins by legal aid, that count in the preparation of a defence case, not the merits of the situation. But even with the best of lawyers and unlimited funds the accused could not stand in the same position as the Crown. Defence agents do not have forensic laboratories and teams of experts at their disposal, or the legal powers of search and detention available to the police. At best, placing the onus of proof on the Crown is not so much an advantage to the accused as a compensation for the unequal start in producing cases. There could be no pretence that accused and Crown start off on an equal footing unless a public system of defence was set up in parallel to the public system of prosecution.

There is therefore an expectation grounded on notions of fairness that any information discovered that is favourable to the accused should be provided to the defence. Lawyers feel this simply does not happen: 'The police don't help. They give you a list of witnesses but of course you don't know what the witnesses said to them. They select and omit to tell you bits that might help your case.'

This is partly an informal process of normal selective perception. People see what they are looking for and policemen who have taken a case as far as charge are, as one policeman put it, 'all out for conviction'. They are looking for incriminating evidence and they do not necessarily know what the defence case is. If the prosecution only turns up black points, not grey or white ones, it is only what you would expect as the informal product of a formal system of adversary investigation. Indeed this has been recognised by Scottish judges:

> The people who take precognitions are searching for evidence in order to prove a crime, and what they take down or afterwards remember of what has been said to them is apt to be coloured by their desire to make out a good case. (*Cook* v. *McNeill*, 1906)

This tendency might be enhanced by the fact that it is the policemen on the case who normally take statements from witnesses in summary cases, and occasionally (though the job is then officially the fiscal's) in jury cases. The Thomson report recognised the problem involved, but also recognised that time and staff did not allow the fiscals to do all this work themselves and that, if 'it is found necessary for the police to continue to assist with this work, it is preferable that an officer familiar with the case should precognosce the witness' (Thomson, 1975, p. 110). Given that, it would seem sensible to allow the accused access to the information culled by the prosecution in order to assess its value for himself. But this does not happen. When it was proposed to the Thomson Committee that witnesses' statements should be exchanged—not, as it happened, to help the accused know the case and spot useful information, but 'to save the time of witnesses, especially the police, and facilitate pleas of guilty'—this was rejected on the grounds that confidentiality would be breached and people would be less willing to help the police (Thomson, 1975, p. 91), while the present situation is explained in Renton and Brown (1972), the official manual of Scots criminal lawyers, in the same vein: 'Confidentiality of Crown precognitions is, in general, necessary for the prosecution of crime' (p. 54). The effect on defences *against* that prosecution is not considered.

Even the passing on of information by the prosecution is not a right, and the exchange of names stretches only to those selected as witnesses, not the whole pool of people interviewed as potential witnesses whose contribution was discarded as not helpful to the prosecution. In England the names of all witnesses interviewed by the prosecution, not just those selected as supporting the prosecution case, should in law (according to the 1967 Criminal Justice Act, *R. v. Bryant and Dixon*, 1946) be passed on to the defence. But the statements they make need not in law be passed on (*R. v. Bryant and Dixon*) and, according to the Fisher Report on the *Confait* case, as a matter of informal policy, they are only provided if the defence ask for them (Fisher, 1977, p. 239). Hence Fisher recommends that disclosure should be made whether or not it is asked for, and, to introduce a little more control, that the Director of Public Prosecutions should play a more active role. The defence does have a right to see the names of the witnesses on the indictment—but not to be provided with addresses by which to contact them (*R. v. Gordon*, 1842).

The Fisher Report also provides a striking—and official— example of just how much filtering of information goes on in the collection of police evidence, and its effects. One of the crucial factors in the ability of the prosecution to produce a strong case out of thoroughly dubious information in the *Confait* case was the role of the police in investigating and reporting the matter. Far from seeking out information for both sides as the law assumes them to do, the police agreed that after confessions were obtained from the three boys, 'enquiries continued only to strengthen the evidence against them' (Fisher, 1977, p. 203). This was despite the fact that there were very definite doubts about the truth of the confessions, brought up at the inquiry, but simply not pursued by the police:

(a) the lack of supporting evidence;

(b) the low intelligence of at least two of the boys;

(c) the fact that to their knowledge there were others (Goode being the principal one) who might have had a motive to kill Confait and who had no alibi for the relevant time;

(d) the apparent discrepancy between the estimates of time of death and the sequence of events described in the boys' statements;

(e) the bizarre nature of the events described by the boys; and

(f) the questions which the statements might have been expected to provoke—how could the boys have got in and out, and done what they described doing, undetected? How did they know which was Confait's room? Why should they go to a lighted room to steal? How could they have killed Confait without disturbing the room? How did they find the flex and why did they put it back in the drawer where according to Goode it was normally kept? What happened to the handbag? (Fisher, 1977, p. 203)

Statements taken from witnesses by the police *were* given to the defence, but they were edited versions only. Two sets of statements were taken: the first were full accounts, including information favourable to the defence, the second were short versions presenting only pro-prosecution information. Only the latter were given to the defence. The police were thus able to comply with policy by providing witnesses' statements and at the same time protect their own distorted case by making sure they excluded information that might point to the innocence of the accused (Fisher, 1977, p. 230).

What is more, the written police report to the Director of Public Prosecutions presented a much harder case against the three youths than all the information available could suggest. This was done by adding into the official statements points helpful to the prosecution case which were not mentioned in the record of interrogation, by misrepresenting the evidence on when the murdered man had last been seen and by omitting points helpful to the defence such as the improbabilities in the confessions and the fact that there had been another suspect (Fisher, 1977, pp. 210–12).

The crucial issue in the case was timing: the boy who confessed to the murder had an incontrovertible alibi for what emerged on appeal as the actual time of death. But in the police report timing was fudged. Indeed Fisher (1977) concludes that 'far from trying to make the time of death more precise, those concerned with the investigation and prosecution . . . made every effort to keep it as vague as possible' (p. 20). There was simply no reference to the boys' movements, the disagreements between the experts on time of death or the discrepancy, 'plain as a pikestaff' (p. 23), between the confessions and the experts' estimates. What is more, the time of death recorded on the crime report was mysteriously altered from 'between 7 p.m.–11 p.m.' to '7 p.m.–1.30 a.m.', with 1.30 a.m. written over the original time (p. 196), so obviating any problems with an alibi which extended only to 11.30 p.m. The case was thus strengthened as it was processed by transforming or omitting evidence that might raise reasonable doubts.

The *Confait* case demonstrates very clearly how ambiguous information can be filtered into an unambiguous case, and how points that raise doubts, helpful to the accused but available only to the police, may never come to light. It also demonstrates exactly why Royal Commissions and committees on criminal procedure should not assume only defence cases are susceptible to 'fabrication' and 'adjustment'.

In two special cases, the prosecutor has access to information that the defence has not, simply by virtue of representing and using the power of the state. One is access to police records and so to information on any previous convictions the accused or other witnesses may have.[2] The second is access to documentary evidence. The police have available to them powers of search and removal which the defence has not. If the accused requires documents for his case, for example account books in a case of embezzlement, either from a third party or from the prosecutor, he cannot compel the possessor to hand them over but must take out a civil case of diligence, with all the expense that entails, to appeal for the right to see and use them. Though Renton and Brown (1972, p. 80) say 'such applications have been repeatedly granted' they are far from being cut and dried. In *Hassan* v. *H.M.Adv.* (1971) Lord Cameron rejected the taken-for-granted view that a statement from the defence lawyer to say the documents were required for the case would be sufficient grounds for granting the application. Rather some indication of their role in the proposed defence was required. Documentary evidence thus becomes available only at the expense of disclosing the defence case.

So the doctrine of 'no surprise' seems to work more for the prosecution than for the defence. Nowhere is this more obvious than in the procedures regarding special defences. These are alibi, self-defence, insanity, incrimination of a specified other person, and, oddly, 'that the accused was asleep at the time when he committed the crime charged'. In these instances prior notice must be given to the prosecutor at committal. If notice is given later he is entitled to an adjournment for further investigation into the claimed defence. In short the Crown's positive case remains something to speculate upon from the bare list of witnesses. But when the defence offers a positive case the prosecutor is not left to put two and two together from interviews with defence witnesses, but is provided with a right to prior notice about the case he will have to counter. Information on both sides of the dispute is more readily available to the Crown.

## POWER OVER WITNESSES

Information alone, however, is not enough. Evidence must be presented at the trial orally, on oath or affirmation by first-hand witnesses, so that part of the preparation of a case is inevitably the task of finding people who are competent and willing to put the relevant information to the court. When it comes to procedural powers over witnesses the same imbalance is revealed.

The prosecutor's role as agent of the state provides both the aura and the sanctions of official authority. Potential witnesses for the prosecution are approached either by a uniformed policeman, or by an equally official warrant of citation from the court. Potential witnesses for the defence are approached by the accused himself, his solicitor, or by the solicitor's assistants. The latter are often ex-policemen as it happens, but lack the authority of uniforms just as the accused and the solicitor lack the compulsion of officialdom. Being a witness is an experience but it is no fun. As one woman put it: 'I was terrified up there. My legs were quaking.' Time at work is lost and expenses are meagre. One sheriff informed the jury they should collect the expenses they were allowed 'within the wholly inadequate limits' (Case 93). Unless the witness had some positive urge to contribute there is no obvious rationality in volunteering for the job, and there can be major disincentives. In Case 93 a young man was accused of brandishing a sword. It was an ornamental brass Indian sword and his story was that he was on his way to sell it to a friend. The friend was not there as a witness, something the prosecutor made good use of:

| Prosecutor: | Why is he not here? |
|---|---|
| Accused: | He was scared. |
| Prosecutor: | You mean you said "Tell them I was going to sell it to you," and he was scared? |
| Accused: | No sir. |
| Prosecutor: | Why was he scared then? |
| Accused: | He was scared cos he was gonnae buy a sword. |
| Prosecutor: | But you can buy them in shops, it was just for hanging on the wall, why was he scared? |

The irony here of course was that the reason he might be afraid was self-evident in the accused's plight.

Not that volunteering may be in issue. Once on the witness list a witness can be forced to attend and indeed punished in a variety of ways if he does not. Thus in Case 96 where one of the victims in a pub brawl was called to give evidence and found to have gone off for lunch without asking permission, the judge prepared for his return by saying to the prosecutor:

> We must decide what we're going to do. Whether you want to charge him with subverting the course of justice by not appearing or whether I charge him with contempt of court.

When the errant did return and came in to court to, as he thought, give evidence, he found himself seized by two policemen, led to the dock, sentenced to imprisonment for contempt of court and led off in handcuffs, stunned and protesting, to the cells. In fact he was released later that afternoon but the whole display demonstrated very clearly the powers of the court over witnesses.

Before forcing a witness to attend and give evidence, however, one would want to know what he is going to say, and that is the purpose of the pre-trial interview or 'precognition'. Calling him to court without interviewing him first would be to risk him actually giving evidence against, rather than for, your own side. But in Scotland this is exactly the dilemma the defence—and only the defence—faces. If a potential witness for the Crown refuses to attend for precognition or to give information 'within his knowledge' he is liable to a £25 fine or up to twenty days in prison in accord with the Summary Jurisdiction (Scotland) Act 1954 s. 33(4). No such sanctions are available to the accused. He can cite an unwilling witness to attend court but cannot compel that he be interviewed beforehand, as the prosecution can. To cite him on force of law as a witness would therefore be to do so blindly and take the risk of adverse evidence. The Thomson Committee (1975) recommend that the defence be given the right to seek a warrant to cite a witness for precognition (p. 91). For the moment, the informal advantages of state authority behind the prosecution are bolstered by the one-sided nature of formal sanctions.

Particular situations can make things even more difficult. For example, the accused's position regarding witnesses may be complicated further by the procedures of group trials. The magistrates' courts in particular are dominated by offences against public order, like breach of the peace. Offences like these often involve several individuals who 'formed a noisy crowd outside a public house' or are charged with brawling with each other, and they are tried together. Normally the only witnesses are the police and the group of accused people. In this situation the accused who disputes that he was part of the crowd, or that he was contributing to the noise, or says he was trying to stop the brawl has no witnesses other than his co-accused to rely on for a case. But Scots law states that an accused cannot call a co-accused to give evidence even with his consent, and he cannot normally cross-examine him when he is giving evidence for his own case. The Thomson Report recommends that one defendant should be allowed to call another as a witness so long as the latter agrees. But there are further obstacles too.

To give this evidence the co-accused would have to give up his own right to silence and incriminate himself by admitting to being part of the crowd or brawl, while it would also lay him open to questions on previous convictions and the like from which a defendant is normally protected. In a separate trial he could give evidence as a witness and it would not count against him in his own trial, but in the group trial situation this is impossible. To be a witness is to be a witness for all aspects of the trial, even if it means being a witness against oneself.

Yet the accused has no right to demand a separate trial. That is a matter for the court to decide and the request for a separate trial in order to call a co-accused as a witness is not considered a sufficient reason in law (*Gemmell* v. *McFadyen and MacNiven*, 1928).

The same can happen in more serious cases. Where, for example, two people are charged with robbery and assault and one did not commit the assault, he may only be able to prove his case if his co-accused is prepared to incriminate himself. This is exactly why separate trials are frowned on, of course. Each guilty accused could get off the hook by one taking the sole blame at the other's trial in the knowledge that it could not be referred to at his own. This would clearly present problems for the prosecution, but not to allow it offers equally difficult problems for the accused.

Of course the co-accused is from another perspective the accomplice and available to turn Queen's evidence for the prosecution against the other defendant. Where each side is vying to secure the co-accused as a witness the prosecution is in a much stronger position. For Defendant 1 to take the witness box in favour of Defendant 2 can be to lay *himself* open to a verdict of guilty; to take the witness box for the prosecution can be to buy himself immunity from trial, since the prosecutor has the power to trade security for evidence. This buys him immunity even from legal action by the prosecuted accomplice. When Mr Turner, after being sentenced to seven years for robbery in March 1978, brought a private prosecution for the same crime against the fellow-robber who turned Queen's evidence against him, the case was rejected by the Queen's Bench as 'vexatious and an abuse of the process of the court':

> There was no doubt about the existence or the unfettered nature of the Director of Public Prosecution's powers. And of course, His Lordship also had to take into account the effect on future criminal inquiries and prosecutions. (*Turner* v. *D.P.P.*, 1978)

To secure his co-accused's testimony the defence can thus offer only punishment, but the prosecution can offer rewards.

In all these ways the accused is faced with problems in getting witnesses to support his case. Yet failure to call witnesses is something that can legally be held against him in court, so that he finds himself—as so often in law—in a procedural double-bind—prevented from getting witnesses there, yet held responsible for their appearance and sometimes for their absence. It is a situation which prosecuting lawyers are happy to capitalise on. Numbers of witnesses become a factor in credibility:

| | |
|---|---|
| Prosecutor: | So Mr A. is lying? |
| Accused: | Yes. |
| Prosecutor: | So Mrs A. is lying? |
| Accused: | Yes. |

| Prosecutor: | So your employer is lying? |
| Accused: | Yes, sir. |
| Prosecutor: | So everyone's lying but you? (Case 12) |

In the elements required for assembling a case, knowing the issues, access to evidence, and availability of witnesses, the prosecution has the advantage. Information games in court, and information selection by judges, should be set in the context of pre-trial procedures which operate as filters on the knowledge available at the trial.

There are indeed procedures to ensure that the filtered versions of reality—and only those—are the ones that appear in court. Cases thus appear exaggeratedly strong or weak in court exactly because all the pre-trial negotiation of evidence and the pre-trial failures to gain access to information or secure the co-operation of potential witnesses go unrecorded. All sorts of procedures encourage the public hearing to expose only the end-products of the pre-trial process, for example the policy of accepting without inquiry minutes of admission, that is, the accepted facts as negotiated by the defence and prosecution before the trial. The ways in which agreement is reached are not the business of the court and the points are simply presented as undisputed. If tapes of pre-trial events are introduced they will be discussed before the trial and only any disputed sections actually brought in as evidence for the judge or jury to decide on. The Thomson Committee recommended that such filters and negotiations be encouraged by increasing the time lapse between indictment and first court appearance from six to twenty days and persuading solicitors to:

> use the procedure more extensively. We therefore recommend that the initiative for reaching agreement on these matters should lie with the Crown. (Thomson, 1975, p. 133)

We might note from this that routines for clarifying issues, for all their informal appearances, are grounded in formal policy and procedure.

More generally, the procedures for collecting witnesses' evidence enhance the channelling out of contradictory information. Witnesses are interviewed before a trial and the aforementioned 'precognitions' taken. These are not statements by witnesses but the interviewer's edited version of what was said, neither signed nor usually seen by the witness himself. Though the value of the information will depend on the witness saying what the counsel selects as relevant not just privately, but in court; and though much is made of the rhetoric that the witness is not bound by his precognition, that indeed he has a right to have it destroyed before he gives evidence at trial (Renton and Brown, 1972, p. 398), there are actually ways of encouraging him to present the information wanted and only that. This is partly achieved in court by techniques of examination and cross-examination, but there are also pro-cedural facilities to help witnesses reproduce the prepared pre-trial accounts.

This is particularly obvious with police witnesses' notebooks. Policemen are permitted to 'refresh their memories' by reading from a notebook in the witness box so long as the notes were 'contemporaneous' with the event. Like all legal criteria it is a fairly elastic term, of course. It has come to mean not 'at the same time' as the *Oxford Dictionary* would have it, but 'at the first available opportunity' (*R. v. Simmonds*, 1967), and that has been interpreted as loosely as two weeks later (*R. v. Langton*, 1876). The justification, of course, is the police witness's profession. The police deal with so many cases, and the delay in court proceedings may mean months of other cases before the one in question comes to court. What is perhaps less obvious is that in English law other witnesses may refresh their memories too, though here a nice distinction is drawn between the public and the private faces of the judicial process. According to Archbold's manual on procedures in English law, a witness may only refresh his memory from a document in the witness box, if special requirements are satisfied (Archbold, 1979, p. 513). However, there is no prohibition on him doing exactly the same before he goes into court with no questions asked. It is even acceptable for him to read a statement written for him by someone else so long as he had also read it at a time when the facts were clear in his memory. A Home Office circular (82/1969a) directs that:

> notwithstanding that criminal proceedings may be pending or contemplated, the Chief Officer of police should normally provide a person, on request, with a copy of his statement.

In *R. v. Richardson* (1971) it was noted that this directive had been approved by Lord Parker and the Justices of the Queen's Bench Division, 'the repositories of the Common Law', had endorsed an extension of the practice—of the prosecutor providing these not 'on request' but on his own initiative. Witnesses for the defence are also allowed copies of statements. The chief justification is that otherwise the testimony of the witness becomes a test of memory rather than truthfulness, but it also means—indeed the more so if the memory is so feeble—that it is the filtered version of what the witness had to say at the time edited for a particular black or white case that is being rehearsed before entering the witness box. This might be seen as somewhat defeating the public presentation of a witness's testimony on oath as only what he *directly* experienced.

In addition there are procedural powers that can be brought to bear if witnesses do *not* reproduce pre-trial accounts. In English law, when a witness fails to provide the requisite evidence for the party who called him, the procedures that follow depend on whether he is classified as an unfavourable witness, as it were accidentally failing to be helpful, or wilfully hostile. In general a party may not cross-examine or discredit his own witness, so that if an unfavourable witness fails to reproduce the facts he stated before the trial there is nothing to be done. If the judge classifies the witness as hostile, however, he can be cross-examined and more witnesses can be produced to prove that he has made previous statements inconsistent with what he is saying in court. Indeed the judge can be shown the written record of his previous statement in order to have him classified as a hostile witness (R. Cross, 1974, p. 222).

In Scotland there is no such concept as a hostile witness but there is a right to refer back to previous statements where a witness does not reproduce the account which counsel wants. It is, however, a one-sided right available only to the prosecution, because of a distinction drawn between the records of defence lawyers and prosecutors—precognitions—and the records of the police.

Precognitions were not originally excluded from the 1852 Act which allowed reference to previous inconsistent statements. Indeed in *McNeilie* v. *H.M.Adv.* (1929) it was noted that: 'The statute is extremely generous in its terms and I do not think that any exception has ever been suggested except the case of precognition.' In Scotland precognitions are excepted on the grounds that, first, confidentiality is required for successful prosecution, and second, they are edited versions of interviews:

> filtered through the mind of another whose job it is to put what he
> thinks the witness means into a form suitable for use in judicial

proceedings. This process tends to colour the result. (*Kerr v. H. M. Adv.*, 1952)

It might well be thought, especially after noting police activity in the *Confait* case, that similar arguments could be applied to police statements, but they are not. So, although a witness cannot be attacked in court for failure to fit with the precognition taken by the prosecutor, his credibility can be put in doubt and the pre-trial version brought in as information for the court by putting his police statement to him in examination, as in this case where information was drawn out of very unco-coperative witnesses after a gang fight:

| | |
|---|---|
| Prosecutor: | Do you know McN's sister? |
| Witness: | Yes. |
| Prosecutor: | Did you see her there? |
| Witness: | Never noticed her. |
| Prosecutor: | You realise you're on oath? |
| Witness: | Yes. |
| Prosecutor: | And you're on the Crown list of witnesses? |
| Witness: | Yes. |
| Prosecutor: | But you saw nothing at all? |
| Witness: | I never seen them. |
| Prosecutor: | Have you ever said anything different? |
| Witness: | No. |
| Prosecutor: | I suggest you have. I suggest you told the police that you saw these three accused and the girl coming along just at that point. |

or with another witness:

| | |
|---|---|
| Witness: | I didn't see anyone else. |
| Prosecutor: | Did you give a statement to the police? |
| Witness: | Yes. |
| Prosecutor: | Did you give a description of someone? |
| Witness: | I just saw somebody in a denim jacket. |
| Prosecutor: | So you did see him? |
| Witness: | I only saw arms in a denim jacket. |
| Prosecutor: | And you saw that piece of wood? |
| Witness: | It could've been. |
| Prosecutor: | Were you able to tell the police what happened? |
| Witness: | No. |

| Prosecutor: | Sure? |
| Witness: | Think so, sir. |
| Prosecutor: | Did the police take a note of what you said? |
| Witness: | Yes. |
| Prosecutor: | But you didn't say anything. |
| Witness: | All I saw was something coming down on his head and he fell back into the shop. |
| Prosecutor: | Then why didn't you say so? (Case 98) |

In another case where a victim of assault failed first to identify the knife then to give clear evidence on what had been said during the attack, both prosecutor and judge made it clear they had ways and means of eliciting the information required:

| Prosecutor: | Did he say anything? |
| Witness: | He might have. I couldn't make it out exactly. |
| Prosecutor: | Have you always said that? |
| Witness: | Yes. |
| Prosecutor: | What did you say to the police? |
| Witness: | Oh aye, he said he was going to get me or something. |
| Prosecutor: | Was it not more specific? I'm going to be talking to the policeman you spoke to that night you know, so let us be clear on what you are telling the court. |
| Judge: | Now, Mr S., you have at the moment made two contradictory statements. [Reading] 'I couldn't make it out' and 'he was going to get me or something'. If I think you are prevaricating—do you know what prevaricating means? |
| Witness: | It means, eh, saying something . . . |
| Judge: | [interrupting]: It means avoiding a question. Now if I get the impression you are prevaricating then, believe me, I have powers to use. If you are going to answer, answer truthfully. |

The prosecutor resumes with the now largely intimidated witness:

| Prosecutor: | Did you tell the policeman you were not 100 per cent sure or did you give him two clear sentences? |
| Witness: | (pause) Yes. He said he had a knife for me. He said he'd use it through my heart. (Case 92) |

The right to prove previous inconsistent statements by reference to police statements—and to sanction deviations—thus provides a valuable means of ensuring that the case prepared before the trial is the one produced in court. But since the defence by definition has no police statements but only precognitions to work from, it is available only to the prosecution.

The Thomson Committee, while declining to make precognitions a legitimate subject for examination, nonetheless took note of the 'strong feeling' that:

> so many witnesses who have given precognitions which incriminate an accused depart from their precognitions at the trial that something has to be done to overcome the problem. (Thomson, 1975, p. 166)

They recommended three changes. First, prosecutors should be allowed to recall witnesses after all the evidence is led to prove that statements made to the police contradict testimony brought out by the defence even if this removes from the accused his traditional right to the last word in the trial. Second, in tune with English law, witnesses should be allowed to see their precognitions before the trial to sharpen their memories, even though these are not their own statements but the edited version prepared by prosecutor, defence lawyer, or police. Third, they suggest sharpening up procedure by not only allowing examination related to precognitions on *oath*, but attaching criminal sanctions to any departure from the pre-trial statement, to the tune of up to two years' imprisonment, a fine or both. This sanction would be available only to the Crown. The problem is defined as one 'where the Crown case fails' (Thomson, 1975, p. 168) and to stretch it to the defence too would be to make it 'unnecessarily wide in its application'. This is based on the dubious assumption that:

> almost all Crown witnesses who have incriminated an accused in a sworn statement before a sheriff (and it will be on this incriminatory evidence or at least partly on the basis of this incriminatory evidence that the Crown will have launched its prosecution) will have told the truth in the statement. (Thomson, 1975, p. 169)

So one more one-sided power for the Crown is proposed despite the minority view on the Committee that:

> It seems wrong that a witness . . . should be liable to punishment
> for making a material change from an earlier sworn statement if
> that change helps the defence, but not if it helps the prosecution.
> (Thomson, 1975, p. 171)

The recommendation is, in fact, only a strengthening of a sanction
already in existence—contempt of court by prevarication which is
liable to punishment by a £25 fine or twenty days in prison but can
be 'purged' by giving the evidence required.

In short, in all three elements involved in assembling a case—
knowledge of the issues, access to information, and power over
witnesses—the defence is at a disadvantage compared with the
prosecution in trying to construct a strong positive case. So when it is
triumphantly pointed out that there is an all-too-obvious explanation for the statistical success of prosecution cases at trial, notably
that the pre-trial filters operate such that only indisputably strong
Crown cases come to trial at all, it should be borne in mind that
strong and weak cases do not miraculously appear after an incident
ready formed like tablets of stone on Mount Sinai. They are the
product of a process of construction in which both the technical
skills of lawyers and the structural opportunities and limitations
offered by the legal system play their part in shaping what facts get
into the courts and just how strong or weak a case can be *independent*
of the incident in question.

Examining the niceties of legal procedure suggests that the
strength of the prosecution case at the trial is a product of just such
influences. Adversary investigation filters out ambiguities and
leaves only black and white cases—the caricature versions of reality
offered by prosecution and defence; courtroom powers and sanctions help prevent any deviation in court from either of these filtered
versions, but especially from the Crown case; and the unequal
powers available to the adversaries before the trial help ensure that
the prosecution case is the stronger.

These filters, however, are not observable by the judge or jury,
press or public watching justice being done. They simply see the
prosecutor successfully executing the burden of proving guilt. *How*
that has been organised, out of the public eye, is of necessity
unknown. So it is that the intermeshing of public and private sectors
in the legal process allows the trial to fulfil simultaneously two
functions: the ideological function of displaying the rhetoric of
justice in action by being tipped *visibly* in favour of due process and

the accused, *and* the pragmatic function of crime control by being tipped *invisibly* but decisively in favour of conviction. The role of the trial can only be understood by being set in the context of the legal process as a whole.

# 6 Standing Trial: Prosecutor's Duties, Defendant's Rights?

The rhetoric of justice is expressed not just in the general clichés surrounding the trial but in the specific roles of prosecutor and defendant that follow from them. Whatever the situation may be behind the scenes, once in court the prosecutor seems to be given all the duties and the defendant all the privileges. The rhetoric poses the trial essentially as a test for the prosecutor. The accused need do nothing—it is up to the prosecutor to prove guilt or fail. The 'test' involves five basic tasks for the prosecutor in proving guilt, with attendant rights for the defendant. First, the prosecutor, not the accused, must make the case; the accused can make a case or simply remain silent and the prosecutor may not prove a point by suggesting that silence means guilt. Second, the prosecutor must prove his case without using useful but inadmissible evidence, not, for example, introducing any reference to the defendant's previous convictions although the defendant can always attack the credibility of a prosecution witness on this basis. Third, the prosecutor must prove *guilt*, which normally includes intent. Fourth, he must reach a minimum standard of what legally constitutes sufficient evidence for a conviction, and the accused may always close the case by submitting he has not done so. Fifth, he must pass the crucial *subjective* test of convincing the jury beyond reasonable doubt that his evidence is true. But the powers and privileges of the trial have proved as open as previous stages of the criminal process to qualification by case law and statute, and these tasks are not always quite so demanding—nor the related defendant's privileges quite so secure—as a general summary suggests. There are ifs and buts attached to every one.

# THE BURDEN OF PROOF AND THE RIGHT TO SILENCE

The Criminal Law Revision Committee's proposal to revoke the defendant's right to remain silent in court, or at least to make it subject to adverse comment (the Thomson Report recommended the same) sparked off a heated debate, stimulated pamphlets of protest and was seen as one of the crucial reasons for abandoning proposed legislation to reform criminal procedure. Yet it is hard to find the grounds for either side of the debate since in large measure the situation proposed by the Committee already exists in law.

The crucial proposal in the Committee's Report, and indeed in the evidence of Sir David McNee, the Metropolitan Police Commissioner, to the Royal Commission on Criminal Procedure in 1979, is this: if the defendant chooses not to enter the witness box to present his own version of events and to have it tested by cross-examination, then the jury should be able to draw adverse implications from this: they should, in short, be able to infer that silence means guilt. The idea that the current situation differs from this is based on the fact that the 1898 Criminal Evidence Act expressly prohibited the prosecutor from commenting on the accused's silence. The report in the *Guardian* of Sir David's evidence puts it like this:

> Neither prosecuting counsel nor the judge is entitled to draw any inference from the choice of a defendant not to give evidence . . . [and he recommends:] Judges and prosecution should be able to comment on the defendant's silence. (17 January 1979)[1]

This is, however, a somewhat misleading account, since it confuses comment with inference, and conflates the rights of judge, jury, and prosecutor.

The current situation is that the prosecutor should *not* comment at all in his final speech on the defendant's failure to give evidence: neither to draw attention to it, nor to suggest any implications from it. He may of course make great play, as Chapter 3 shows, of the accused's alleged silence on being arrested, or indeed on his alleged pre-trial statements. Silence in court somewhat loses its value if words can be put in the silent mouth via 'verbals' reported from the pre-trial stage. Indeed the Thomson Committee saw the issue of the right to silence in court as a red herring exactly because of the admissibility of pre-trial statements. Instead of:

forcing the accused into the witness box at his trial when he has heard the evidence for the prosecution and is in a position to adjust his own evidence to meet the case against him . . . the best opportunity of obtaining the truth from an accused is immediately after he has been charged when he does not know the evidence against him. (Thomson, 1975, p.188)[2]

The assumed dishonesty of the accused expressed here jars a little with the presumption of innocence, while the recommendation as a whole violates 'the sacred and inviolable' protection from self-incrimination, and the prosecutor's duty to bear the burden of proof beyond reasonable doubt.

The right to silence in court should indeed be set not just in the context of pre-trial silence or statements but in the context of the trial in general. The defendant may have a right to remain silent, to produce no evidence but force the prosecution to prove the case against him. But consider the nature of a trial, with the full prosecution case stated first rather than each issue being debated in full all the way through; the nature of a case, with information selected and distorted to fit into a version of reality favourable to one side only; the nature of the *prosecution* case, setting the agenda for the issues of the case according to the information available and amenable; the nature of cross-examination, too 'bitty' to indicate the defence version, indeed designed not to give away the defence version while the prosecutor is still presenting his, and often, with so little pre-trial knowledge of all the existing evidence, a shot in the dark rather than a knowledgeable prepared attack. Consider these things and it is only too clear that if the prosecution case goes smoothly there can be no reason not to accept it *unless* it is answered. Sometimes this is not left implicit but made only too clear in the closing comments of judges. When a prosecutor expressed anxiety, in coming to the end of his side of the case, that his last witness had not yet turned up, the sheriff—sitting without a jury—announced nonchalantly: 'I wouldn't worry. You've plenty of evidence for the first charge and the second is immaterial in comparison.' (Case 96). Or again, when a prosecutor proposed calling a witness to clarify a point at the end of his evidence and before the defence case, the sheriff responded: 'Well can we have him for that only because I'm satisfied otherwise.' The defence counsel protested: 'Your honour!' And the sheriff only then qualified his acceptance of the prosecution case: 'Subject to any evidence led by the defence.' (Case 95).

Indeed the defendant's right not to prove his innocence but to let the prosecutor prove his guilt, should be set in the context of the criminal process not just, as we have seen in Chapter 5, in terms of how that process affects the reality of the burden of proof, but of how it affects the reality of the presumption of innocence. Criminal procedure includes a filter between the police and the court for the specific purpose of establishing that there is a prima facie case for conviction before prosecutions are brought to trial. The procurator fiscal's discretion to drop or pursue police cases fulfils this function in Scotland, the magistrates' decision in committal proceedings does the same in indictments in England. The filter is not so efficient in practice that only watertight cases come to trial, while 'watertight cases' as we have seen are themselves only an artificial construction. Indeed Baldwin and McConville (1979) found that most defendants were committed for trial without the prosecution case being scrutinised either by the defence (they were given the prosecution papers only on the day of committal) or indeed by the magistrates, who did not look at the evidence (p. 25). But the presupposition that there is an established case for conviction is thus built into the assumptions of the court before any evidence is heard.[3] If then the accused enters the court on a rhetorical presumption of innocence but a real presumption of guilt, it is hardly surprising. The displacement is not just the product of common-sense assumptions that where there is smoke there is fire, the work routines of the court officials (Carlen, 1976) or the symbolic position of the accused in the dock (Hetzler and Kanter, 1974). After all there is something a little tautological in that. Being in the dock does not intrinsically mean guilt. Rather it means that to the observer because it has become associated with conviction, but presumably moving the defendant to a table or a pulpit would soon come to have the same connotation. It is the status of being a defendant rather than his location that implies guilt. Routine expectations and symbolisms may play their part in replacing the presumption of innocence with a presumption of guilt, but it is also built into a system of pre-trial procedures which implies that the innocent (and the guilty who cannot be proved guilty) are exempted from the process of public proof. In short, the very fact that a case has come to trial at all means *in law* that the prosecution case is recognised as having some convincing if preliminary proof of the defendant's guilt.

More specifically, prohibiting the prosecutor from commenting on the accused's silence in court, does not mean that the judge or jury may not infer guilt from it, or take account of it in weighing up the case for conviction. As a Scottish case puts it:

> . . . the silent defendant does take a risk and if he fails to challenge evidence given by witnesses for the Crown by cross-examination or, in addition, by leading substantive evidence in support of his challenge, he cannot complain if the court not merely accept that unchallenged evidence but also, in the light of all the circumstances, draw from it the most unfavourable and adverse inference to the defence that it is capable of supporting. (*McIlhargey* v. *Herron*, 1972)

Indeed the prohibitions placed on the prosecutor from commenting on the accused's silence are not repeated for the judge. Whether or not the 1898 Act was intended to prohibit comment from anyone in court on the accused's silence, only the prosecutor was *explicitly* prohibited from doing so and English case law the following year fastened on this literal interpretation to establish that the *judge* is quite entitled to draw the jury's attention to the accused's silence in court—indeed from his position of neutrality and authority he may arguably do so with greater impact that the prosecutor could. This was defined as part of his role in commenting on the evidence and on how the case has been conducted(*R.* v. *Rhodes*, 1899), and precisely how he commented was left to the judge's own discretion, normally, as Heydon (1975) puts it 'in robust terms' (p. 153). In Scotland in 1946 it was noted that judges should not put 'undue emphasis' on the accused's silence (*Scott*) and in England in 1950, it was suggested that judges ought to be careful (*Waugh* v. *R.*, 1950), although emphasis was laid on the specific 'state of the evidence' in that particular case, where the prosecution had an extremely weak case (the police had actually dropped it because there was so little evidence and it only went to court at all on the direction of the coroner). In such circumstances it was considered a bit excessive for the judge to comment on the accused's silence nine times in the course of the summing up when it was far from clear that the prosecution had really made out a case against him anyway.

Where the prosecution case seems strong, however, the judge's right to comment may even become, in the Court of Appeal's words in 1973, (paralleled in Scotland in 1974[4]) a duty:

> In the judgment of this court, if the trial judge had not

commented in strong terms on the appellant's absence from the witness box, he would have been failing in his duty . . . where an accused person elects not to give evidence, in most cases but not all, the judge should explain to the jury what the consequences of his absence from the witness box are . . . (*R.* v. *Sparrow*, 1973)

The judge's duty to *comment* does not mean he may himself explicitly *infer* guilt from the accused's silence, nor direct the jury to do so,[5] but he is quite entitled to tell the jury that any innocent explanations from the defence lawyer would have come better from the accused, who would have been liable to cross-examination,[6] or remind them that they are there to represent the common sense of ordinary people and instruct them to follow that common sense in drawing what implications they consider fit from the accused's silence. He may indeed suggest what questions their common sense might dictate to them. The jury is thus directed it may if common sense so dictates, infer reasons for silence that suggest guilt despite the fact that there may be many others. The law does specify that there should be 'no *apparent* reason for silence other than inability to answer truthfully the case made' (Heydon, 1975, p. 156) but there may be many unknown factors quite consistent with innocence involved. The jury is *not* warned about inferring too much.

Indeed it is interesting that the jury *is* specifically directed to follow 'common sense' rather than legal rules. Rather than directing jurors to ask why the defendant has remained silent, the judge could just as readily have a duty to tell them they need not and may not ask such questions: silence is a right and as such can be exercised without explanation, the jury must be persuaded by the prosecutor's case not the defendant's silence. It is often claimed that there would be no point in directing the jury like this because they would operate on their common sense anyway. This not only assumes a rather one-sided view of 'common sense', but overlooks the possibility that jurors operate not as ordinary members of the public moved by common sense but as legal actors deciding according to legal rules[7]—legal rules which in this case they are being told to ignore. Jurors in short do not informally break the rules by jumping to 'common sense' conclusions from the defendant's silence: they are explicitly directed by the judge to operate in direct contradiction to the legal rhetoric of the right of silence.

The judge, of course, must choose his words carefully. He must not suggest, even 'by a slip of the tongue' (*R.* v. *Sparrow*, 1973) that the accused *must* speak if the defence is to succeed. Even this, however, does not apply to everyone. Statutes and case law have created offences and legal doctrines which undermine not only the right of silence but the presumption of the defendant's innocence and the placing of the burden of proof on the prosecution. Indeed, Ashworth argues that so many qualifications have been imposed on the *Woolmington* v. *D.P.P.* principle—and he cites in particular the 1952 Magistrates' Courts Act and the case of *Edwards* (1975) which effectively extended its provisions to the Crown Courts—that:

> the golden thread has become tarnished. English law now so frequently imposes upon the defendant the burden of proving a particular defence that it cannot be asserted with confidence whether the hallowed presumption of innocence or the disowned presumption of guilt is the dominant principle—which in reality is the rule and which the exception. (Ashworth, 1978, p. 385)

One way in which this is done is via the notion of legal presumptions. 'Innocent till proved guilty' may be the only presumption that has reached the rhetoric and become one of the common catch-phrases about justice, but it is not the only presumption in law. There are all sorts of practical items like how long it takes from conception to birth which can simply be presumed rather than proved, a convenient time-saving device. But the convenience has also stretched in some circumstances beyond saving time about proving practical items of that sort into something of a rather different order, not just making it easier to prove guilt but eliminating the need for proof altogether.

So according to the 1968 Theft Act if someone is caught carrying tools that could be used for a burglary—and that of course raises questions of definition—it is not, as we have seen,[8] up to the police to prove that he did use the tools for a burglary or that he intended to do so, as the rhetoric of the burden of proof on the prosecution might suggest. Rather it is up to the arrestee to explain himself if he is not to be automatically presumed guilty. Likewise according to the 'doctrine of recent possession' if the accused is found with stolen goods not long after they were stolen, and in incriminating circumstances, he is assumed to be guilty of theft or receiving unless *he* can raise doubts to the contrary.

A perfectly logical reason is offered for this departure from the 'golden thread' of the law. Presumptions allow the law to do the impossible:

one of their principal uses being to establish facts which, by their nature, are incapable of proof by direct evidence. (Walker and Walker, 1975, p. 50)

And so useful are they indeed that, according to Walker and Walker's text on evidence in Scotland:

the presumption of innocence, for example, which is a *presumptio juris*, is displaced in the courts, as a matter of everyday occurence . . . (Walker and Walker, 1975, p. 52)

The result is that the accused is faced with proving his innocence and indeed with trying to prove lack of guilty intention; an extremely difficult thing to do. Indeed the law of evidence recognises it as such and generally operates by the rule that no one should be required to prove something was *not* the case; rather the burden of proof should fall on the person who says it was. This has been described in English law as:

an ancient rule founded on considerations of good sense and it should not be departed from without strong reasons. (*Joseph Constantine Steamship Line Ltd* v. *Imperial Smelting Corporation Ltd*, 1942)

The same line is taken in Scotland in discussing the rules of evidence 'of which one of the most fundamental and most rational is *semper praesumitur pro negante*.' (*Lennie* v. *H.M.Adv.*, 1946). This is the justification for the prosecutor not being required to prove for example that a poacher is operating without a licence; rather the accused must prove he has one. The reason is that otherwise the result would be 'many offenders escaping conviction' (*R.v.Turner*, 1816). But the same reasoning does not seem to apply in leaving the accused, in some circumstances at least, not only to have to demonstrate his innocence but to have to do so by proving a negative.

So far as the right of silence is concerned, the accused in these situations has no such privilege, since he must offer an explanation of what he was doing with the tools, or how he came by the stolen goods—or be convicted. So Lord Devlin could point out that in cases of recent possession:

the fact that an accused is found in possession of property recently

stolen does not of itself prove that he knew of the stealing.
Nevertheless it is not open to the accused at the end of the
prosecution's case to submit that he has no case to answer; he
must offer some explanation to account for his possession. . . .
(*Hill* v. *Baxter*, 1958)

Likewise in a Scottish case of a fraud where the accused claimed an
inheritance on the grounds that he had been married to the
deceased lady, had witnesses of a sort to support his story, but did
not give evidence himself, the Lord Justice Clerk could sum up to
the jury in no uncertain terms:

> The one man who might have told us his story is true is sitting
> there. He has preferred the security of the dock to the insecurity of
> the witness box. . . . Now, there are certain cases in which the
> proved facts may raise a presumption of guilt, and in which, in
> the absence of some explanation by the person accused—where
> the person accused is the only one person who can know the real
> truth—a jury may be entitled to draw an inference of guilt; and I
> direct you in law that this is one of them . . . there is evidence
> pointing to it being a dishonest and a fraudulent claim and there
> is no evidence pointing to it being an honest and genuine
> claim. . . . I direct you that there is ample evidence in this case, if
> you accept it, to justify you in finding a verdict of guilty.
> (*H.M.Adv.* v. *Hardy*, 1938)

The defendant's silence in court thus becomes a significant factor in
proving him guilty.

The right of silence then, although it is a phrase that has been
given much mileage in debates about civil rights, is in fact
something of a misnomer. It might be more accurate to describe it as
the recognition that without torture no one can now be forced to
speak in court. To suggest that it is currently a privilege which the
defendant can legitimately exercise without fear of adverse consequences is quite misleading. Certainly he may remain silent in or
out of court, but in contradiction to the rhetoric of the presumption
of innocence and the burden of proof, guilt may be presumed in
some cases, inferred in others, if he does: the defendant's silence in
court as readily as out of it is less a privilege and an obstacle to
proving guilt than a fact which may help convict him.

# THE DEFENDANT'S CHARACTER

One of the categories of inadmissible evidence most clearly presented as one-sided, as a problem for the prosecutor, privilege for the accused, is the rule governing information on 'character'.

Discrediting the testimony of any opposing witness plays an important part in the advocate's role of persuading judge or jury to believe his case rather than his opponent's. Discrediting the *character* of an opposing witness is a useful way of doing this, most decisively of all, by showing he has a criminal record. For the prosecutor there is an obstacle: *he* may not bring out as evidence any previous record the accused may have. For the defence, on the other hand, it is always possible to attack the character of a prosecution witness or indeed cross-examine him on his criminal record – for prosecution witnesses may have 'bad characters' too, a point 'common sense' proposals to bring in all relevant information often overlooks. Yet it would be misleading to sum up the situation too readily as one of privileges for the accused, problems for the prosecution. It can equally operate in reverse.

One problem for the defence is simply unequal access to information. Only the prosecutor has official access to police records. To describe the defence position as a privilege is to ignore the fact that he can be in a 'Catch-22' situation with the right to take the initiative on information he is not allowed to have. In English law where a prosecution witness is known to have previous convictions or a 'bad character', it is the duty of the prosecutor to let the defence know this; he can then bring this information out in court and let the jury use it in assessing the credibility of the prosecution witness. However the prosecutor is under no duty to actually check out the character of his witnesses (*R. v. Collister and Warhurst*, 1955) while, if the prosecutor does *not* pass on the relevant information, he is not necessarily sanctioned and a conviction may well be sustained on appeal (*R. v. Matthews*, 1975). The prosecution is therefore very much in control of the information game on the character of witnesses. That may even include the character of the defendant. In English law the prosecutor has a duty to supply the defence with details of the defendant's record, but not in Scotland. In the context of this information control, exercising the defence privilege of attacking bad character can backfire. The defence solicitor may attack a Crown witness in the belief that his client has a clean record, only to find that the accused had been hiding his past, and that the prosecution brings in his previous record as evidence: for the sake of undermining one aspect of the prosecution case the defence agent has jeopardised the accused through revealing him as a legally discredited character.

If the defence position on character involves more problems than the rhetoric might suggest, the prosecutor's often involve less. The prosecutor can always bring in discrediting information about the defendant's past in retaliation should the defence attack a prosecution witness's character or lead evidence to suggest his own respectability. We have already seen in Chapter 4 just how broadly 'attacking the character of a prosecution witness' has been defined in England, if not in Scotland, and how easy it is as a result for the retaliation rule to come into play. Even explaining away fingerprints in a prosecution witness's room by saying he had had a homosexual relationship with him, has been interpreted as an attack by the defendant on that witness's character (*R. v. Bishop*, 1974). There is an equally broad definition of 'leading evidence of his own good character'. In *R. v. Coulman* (1927) the defence was deemed to have led evidence on the defendant's good character by establishing that he was married, had a family, and was in regular employment. The Criminal Law Revision Committee suggest just as wide a definition in the examples they give from past cases:

> One of two men charged with conspiracy to rob (both had long criminal records) went into the witness box wearing a dark suit and looking as if he were a respectable businessman. When asked by his counsel when and where he met his co-accused, he said: 'About eighteen months ago at my golf club. I was looking for a game. The secretary introduced us.' In another case the defence continued to introduce evidence suggesting that the accused, who lived on crime, was negotiating for the purchase of a substantial property. (Criminal Law Revision Committee, 1972, para. 135)

This provides some interesting insights into the assumptions and biases of the Criminal Law Revision Committee: middle-class lifestyle and criminal behaviour are apparently assumed to be incompatible—though studies of white-collar crime might well suggest the opposite—and crime is something expected only of the lower class. However it also suggests that the accused may not even dress in his Sunday best without it being taken as a sanctionable tactic allowing the prosecutor to introduce supposedly prohibited information of his past record. Indeed cases, not just these comments on cases, support this. In *R.* v. *Hamilton* (1969) the accused, charged with indecent assault, was required to remove a regimental blazer, in case it was considered evidence of good character. Since research has shown that *not* dressing up for court can lead to the implication being drawn that he is *not* respectable or indeed not showing respect for the court, with adverse consequences for him too,[9] the accused may be caught, as so often, in a double bind.

There are also indirect ways in which information about the accused can be implied in court as the result of prior procedural rules. Whether the accused is on bail or in custody gives a clue. It does not take a juror of unusual genius to work out that the accused who is brought into court by two uniformed men with H.M.P. on their epaulettes might have come straight from Her Majesty's Prison, and has therefore been adjudged for some reason different from his co-accused transporting himself unaccompanied. Studies[10] have also shown that defendants who have been on bail stand a better chance of acquittal than those who have not, perhaps because they have less opportunity to come smartly turned out for the occasion, perhaps because of the cues suggested by just being in custody. A person can be refused bail for several reasons; one important factor that will weigh against any request for bail is that he has previous convictions. A known criminal has no right to bail. Previous conviction can thus operate at the pre-trial level to feed adverse information about the accused into the court.

More generally, controls are weak. Even where the accused's record has been illegitimately brought out in court, appeals have been turned down if it is deemed to have had no prejudicial effect (*McLean* v. *Skinner*, 1907); it is not a rigidly exclusive rule. It is explicitly overruled too in specific types of offence, notably sex offences, where 'similar acts' or the unusual similarity of style or behaviour in previous cases for which the accused has been convicted, can be used as evidence that he is the culprit this time too. There are obvious dangers here of a vicious circle of being convicted, being prime suspect next time, reconvicted, even more of a prime suspect next time and so on. There are also dangers of deliberate mimicking to pass the blame onto that prime suspect, while it is a procedure quite contrary to the idea that each case should stand on its own merits. According to the Prevention of Crimes Act 1871, section 19, previous convictions may also be called upon to prove intent (*Watson* v. *H.M.Adv.*, 1894), while some laws actually *require* that the accused's previous record be made known to the judge and jury; indeed the charge may be explicitly constituted by suspicious behaviour on the part of someone with a previous conviction. Case 9, for example, arose out of the police observing a 'known thief' and his companion 'taking a special interest in cars', and contrary to the normal expectations that previous convictions are not mentioned in court and the judge or jury certainly does not know of them, it *began* with the stipendiary magistrate addressing one of two co-accused:

> You're the known thief. Do you understand that procedure? Your finger prints have been taken, matched with those taken from you at borstal and you have two previous convictions. Therefore you are a known thief.

In all these ways then the accused's record is less of a privilege for the accused and less of a problem for the prosecutor than a general statement of their positions might suggest.

## PROVING GUILT

The prosecutor's third task involves proving *guilt*, the fourth and fifth tasks *proving* guilt, with the emphasis on each word in turn because each involves problems of definition. In the realm of legal and indeed moral ideas[11] *guilt* involves not just objective but subjective criteria: it means proving that the accused not only *did* some specified deed, but that he *intended* to do it. Intent or *mens rea* is an important part of the ideology of criminality as the ultimate justification of punishment: it ties in with the democratic notion of the rule of law. The common law maxim is *Actus non facit reum nisi mens sit rea*: the deed does not make a man guilty unless his mind be guilty. It is described in Archbold as:

> of fundamental importance in upholding the rule of law. To make a man liable to imprisonment for an offence which he does not know that he is committing and is unable to prevent is repugnant to the ordinary man's conception of justice and brings the law into contempt. (Archbold, 1979, s. 1438 a)

*Mens rea* features as a central chapter in books on criminal law, especially 'the general part' on the theories behind it. Yet it receives remarkably little attention in the books on evidence, an indication that the ideology of criminal law and the pragmatics of criminal procedure do not always go hand in hand. There is little on the topic in the books on evidence because there is effectively nothing to say. The existential problems of proving intent that pose such fascinating problems for theorists of crime and criminal law are frequently sidestepped and the concept of *mens rea* effectively rendered redundant by routinely[12] collapsing intent and behaviour together:

> . . . corrupt and evil intent (*mens rea*), is a necessary element in crimes. . . . It is inferred, however, from proof of the crime itself, and does not need to be separately established. (Walker and Walker, 1975, p. 25)

What is more the concept does not apply in many offences at all. For some it is ruled out by the doctrine of strict liability. In others, as we have seen in Chapter 3, effect, indeed *potential* effect, rather than intent is all that need be suggested, while evidence of intent, from the cases observed seems to boil down to the policeman's impression. In English law, the declaration in *R*. v. *Tolson* (1889) that the defendant has to prove facts from which the jury might reasonably infer that she had reasonable grounds for believing her action legitimate, became the basis, according to Archbold (1979) for a particular concept of proof of intent. *Mens rea* came to mean

> the absence of an honest and reasonable belief in the existence of circumstances which if true, would make the act or omission for which the accused is indicted innocent. (Archbold, 1979, s.14:38(9)

The emphasis on 'absence' effectively switched the burden to the accused to prove such honest belief was present (a relocation of the burden of proof which lasted till the *Woolmington* decision of 1935); the emphasis on 'reasonable' switched the *subject* of proof from what the accused *actually* thought at the time to the more objective standard of what a reasonable man in the same circumstances might have thought, a total undermining of the notion of intent.

The objective standard was at that time the only sensible one anyway since defendants could not give evidence themselves of their subjective state of mind, or for that matter anything else, until 1898. The Criminal Evidence Act of that year changed that situation but the objective interpretation of *mens rea* lingered on, and only recently has there been a small move towards a more subjective approach, that is, to advising acquittal if the jury accepts that the defendant honestly believed what he was doing was right, whether there were reasonable grounds for his belief or not (*R. v. Smith*, 1974).

More generally, the linking of intent with the idea of *known* law is ruled out by the fact that citizens are *presumed* to know the law anyway, whether they actually do or not—ignorance of the law is no defence against intent even for a foreigner—and indeed they are presumed to know they are committing a particular *type* of offence, whether they actually do or not. It is, for example, no defence for a person accused of assaulting a police officer in the execution of his duty that he did not *know* he was a police officer (unidentified and in plain clothes) executing his duty (Archbold, 1979, p. 1439d). Even shooting X accidentally while aiming at Y is not deemed accidental but intentional via the doctrine of 'transferred malice'.

*Proving* guilt involves both objective and subjective aspects too. The law distinguishes between credibility of evidence, the jury's subjective decision, and sufficiency of evidence whereby the judge first decides whether the evidence, regardless of how credible it is, meets minimum *objective* legal standards. The defence indeed has a right to challenge the prosecution case for failing to meet the objective standards of legal sufficiency, and submit that there is no case to answer.

To do so, however, can be a dangerous strategy. If successful it ends the case. But if it is unsuccessful it means that the defence case begins with an explicit—if legally limited—statement from the judge that he has decided after hearing the prosecution case that there is evidence for the jury to consider (*R. v. Falconer-Atlee*, 1974), in short that the prosecution has established a prima facie case. The jury is therefore given an explicit favourable conclusion to the prosecution case and an unfavourable cue for its reception of defence evidence.

That is in England. In Scotland the consequences are more direct and immediate. If the claim of no case to answer is unsuccessful the next step is a verdict of guilt with no opportunity to lead evidence for the defence at all, since the accused can only choose one strategy or the other: claim no case to answer *or* claim the right to offer a positive case in response, but not both. To try one is therefore to forfeit the other, a situation described to the Thomson Committee (who propose reforming it) as: 'a cruel dilemma and an invidious and unfair position in which to place the defence'. (Thomson, 1975, p. 183)

The effect of this is demonstrated by Case 91, where a man was stopped while driving a car stolen three weeks previously and charged with theft or receiving. At the end of the prosecution case the defence counsel declared to the judge that he did not propose to lead evidence. As an observer at that time unread in procedural law, I took this to mean that the defence counsel was afraid to put the accused in the witness box for fear of what he might say to incriminate himself—and that may also have been the case. But set now in the context of legal rules it is clear from what followed that the defence counsel, whether he wanted to put his client in the witness box or not, was caught in just this dilemma, for in the absence of the jury he went on to submit that there was insufficient evidence and no case to answer. His point was that in order to make his case, the prosecutor had to prove incriminating circumstances to suggest that the accused knew he was guilty, and that this had not been done. But the judge decided that there was a case to be put to the jury, and there followed a verdict of guilty.

This case demonstrates three dangers for the defence in submitting there is no case to answer. First in presenting his submission to the judge he has to disclose the criticisms of the prosecution case that he will be making. The prosecutor thus goes into his final speech to the jury forearmed and the defence counsel effectively loses the advantage of having the last word. Second, in Scots law at least, he loses the possibility of producing evidence for the accused. Third, the discussion takes place in the absence of the jury and the reasons for there being no defence evidence—and indeed for the accused himself not speaking—are not given to the jury. They are therefore left to assume it to be a matter of choice and an indication of guilt rather than a constraint imposed by legal rules. The defendant thus has a right to challenge rather than dispute the prosecutor's case; but as is so often the case with the rights of the accused, it is a right with drastic penalties attached.

There are no statistics on how often a submission of no case to answer succeeds, but it would be surprising if it happened very often for the simple reason that the minimum legal demands imposed by the concept of sufficiency are, as we have seen in Chapter 2, often rather lower than one might expect. The amount of evidence required for conviction in England has never been very demanding. Indeed, Langbein argues that it was precisely because the standard of proof was so low in England that for most of its history it has not involved torture. The high demands of the European jurisdictions on what constituted enough evidence to prove a case, led them to acquire it by torture; England did not need to (Langbein 1977, p. 77). There was and still is no need for corroboration in the majority of cases. As Langbein puts it:

> To this day an English jury can convict a defendant on less evidence than was required as a mere precondition for interrogation under torture on the continent. (Langbein 1977, p. 78)

One witness has always constituted sufficient evidence in common law for a conviction, and that remains true if the witness is an accomplice and indeed even if he has the very strong incentive of being offered a pardon on condition that the defendant is convicted.[13] Juries should normally be warned about the reliability of accomplice evidence, though even that is not done in joint trials (Renton and Brown, 1972, p. 380) and joint trials are normal where co-accused are involved—indeed the rules are such that it is extremely unusual for a defendant to be tried alone, even if he requests it.[14] Even a direct witness is not really necessary in England for legal sufficiency: an uncorroborated alleged confession will do. The effects of this are graphically illustrated by the *Confait* case in which a finding of guilt was based on the uncorroborated alleged confession of a mentally retarded teenager interviewed without a solicitor or his parents—a confession which was later proved impossible, but only after he and his two co-accused had spent two years in institutions.

In all cases in Scotland, and in some in England, there *is* an objective criterion of sufficiency: corroboration. Scotland is often described as having a tougher standard of proof because of its insistence on corroboration, but of course it also has the corollary of a third verdict, 'not proven', which somewhat undermines this. Rather than upholding its tough rules by finding anyone whose guilt is not proved according to their demands not guilty, Scots law effectively proclaims that he would have been found guilty if only it was not for those stringent rules: he is not 'not guilty'; the case is simply 'not proven'. In any case the rules are not quite so stringent as they might seem. In both countries the meaning of corroboration has been watered down over the years. The rule according to Renton and Brown's manual 'does not require every circumstance to be proved by two witnesses'. Indeed such is the erosion that has occurred that this manual, listing the 'facts' which do not require corroboration, can state: 'it may be that the only fact of which we can say that it must always be corroborated is the identity of the accused' (Renton and Brown, 1972, pp. 390–1). (This, it may be said, involves pointing him out in the dock, not the most difficult identification procedure, and where this does fail the evidence of two policemen that the defendant was identified earlier, so long as the witness accepts that he did identify him to the police, will do.) Corroboration once meant two independent witnesses; now it simply requires two circumstances. This is so even where the evidence is wholly circumstantial, so long as there are two circumstances. Corroborating evidence need not point unequivocally to guilt, and where there are similar offences charged, a single witness for each can be taken as corroboration. Indeed despite the accused's right against self-incrimination *he* can provide the prosecutor's necessary corroboration. Fingerprint evidence can provide its own corroboration by simply getting two witnesses to identify the presence of the print! (*Hain* v.*H.M.Adv.*, 1934).

Indeed even the strong corroboration of two witnesses independently giving independent supportive testimony in the witness box, or the weaker notion of this simply adding to credibility, may need closer scrutiny . Police witnesses, for example, are allowed to collaborate on the evidence they give, and decide together on what is to go into their notebooks. This is not just a devious practice among the police but in England at least a legal right. The English manual for criminal procedure notes:

> Nothing could be more natural or proper when two persons have been present at an interview with a third person that they should afterwards make sure that they have a correct version of what was said. (*R.* v. *Bass*, 1953)

Indeed they are quite entitled to use the same notebook in the witness box (*R.* v. *Adams*, 1957; Archbold, 1979, p. 514). In addition, any witness may 'refresh his memory' from a document before giving evidence even if it was written by someone else—for example, from a statement written by the police—so long as he had already read it at the time. (It was noted in a 1976 case (*Worley* v. *Bentley*; Archbold, 1979, p. 255) that it was 'desirable' that the defendant should be informed of this, a marked watering down of the previous situation which took for granted that it was 'obviously essential' this should happen.) If the testimony of two police witnesses or police and other prosecution witnesses is corroboratory then one should hardly be surprised. The idea of corroboration may suggest a more demanding criterion of sufficiency of proof than procedural practice actually involves.

Indeed sufficiency is a shifting standard, for ultimately it seems to boil down to the best evidence available. Reading the qualifications one almost comes away with the impression that the rules stand only for cases that can stand them—where they cannot be met, they are modified. Hearsay is inadmissible, *unless* the direct witness has inconveniently died; then it becomes admissible. Corroboration is essential *unless* the crime is one where only perpetrator and victim are present; then it is weakened to allow similar fact evidence. And so on.

More generally, and indeed more indirectly, the very existence of two hurdles of proof—legal sufficiency and the subjective conviction of the jury—on the face of it a double protection for the accused, can ironically help ease the prosecutor's task of convincing the court of guilt. This is because of the nature of the first hurdle and the processes relating it to the second. The legal standards of the first hurdle are not greatly demanding, as we have seen. However, it is the judge's duty to decide that they have been met and to hand the case to the jury only if he considers this done. This is often made explicit. Indeed in cases where alternative charges have been made, in which for example the ultimate charge will be either theft or receiving—depending on the sufficiency of the evidence stated in court—the judge should pass the case to the jury with an explicit statement that there is in law sufficient evidence for a charge of theft or insufficient evidence for a charge of theft but sufficient for a charge of receiving. Likewise where there is more than one charge, the jury may be directed that they can ignore one, since there is insufficient evidence, but go on with the other: 'I have decided for technical reasons there is insufficient evidence for charge two, so you are only asked to consider charge one' (Case 91). (Note the throwaway phrase 'for technical reasons' and the potential implication of 'real' guilt, technical acquittal.) This means that the jury is presented with the case, buttressed by the ambiguous and complex notion that there is sufficient evidence to convict. They need never, of course, be told there is sufficient evidence to acquit since the rhetoric of the presumption of innocence and burden of proof means only the prosecutor's case has to be put to the test. Likewise, in Scotland in particular where a majority verdict is acceptable from the beginning, the judge in summing up will tell the jury what size of majority is necessary to convict though again, since the presumption of innocence is taken for granted in the *rhetoric*, there need be no explicit reference to acquittal.

In sum, these four prosecution tasks—carrying the burden of proof, making a case without infringing the privileges of the accused, proving intent and meeting the standards of legal sufficiency—and the attendant rights for the accused—on silence, character, claiming no case to answer—are all hedged by qualifications which can modify and even totally erode them. The idea that the trial poses problems for the prosecution and privileges for the accused can all too readily be reversed.

The fifth task for the prosecutor is to convince the jury, though even that subjective decision is, as we have seen in Chapter 2, hedged by external legal provisos, and the jury is well-warned that not all its doubts may be reasonable. That said, however, the fact remains that it is the jury who decide. The rules of evidence, case law, the structure of advocacy and the profession all give way to the ordinary man in the street. It is not the convolutions of legal reasoning that decide the verdict but 'common sense': the jury retires to its own room, to secrecy, with no legal professional to direct it, no criticism allowed of its decision and no need to account to the legal experts on how it was reached. In the end it is not state officials who decide but twelve or fifteen ordinary people.

Yet that is only the image: observing the jury from the inside, observing how it actually operates—or is operated—raises serious doubts about its accuracy. This is dealt with at length in a separate study,[15] but suffice to say here that once in the jury box, the jury is no longer twelve or fifteen ordinary people but a group self-consciously playing the *legal* role of jurors, and a group whose 'common sense' has already been moulded into a sense of legal propriety. What is more the jury can only decide on the basis of the information it is presented with. And this is why it is too simple to separate off the jury's decision from the rules of evidence, case law, advocacy, the role of the judge: these are exactly what limit and shape its verdict. Indeed this is why the trial and the verdict cannot be separated from pre-trial processes. What decision can *reasonably* be reached by the judge or jury or the public audience depends on the information provided for them in court, and that, as we have seen, has been structured, shaped, and filtered before the public stage is ever reached. But to understand the role of trial by jury in the legal system we have to set it not just in the context of the processing of the jury, the processing of evidence, the convolutions of legal reasoning; we must also set it in the context of the legal structure. Trial by jury may be one of the cornerstones of the ideology of justice but it is a rare event in criminal justice. So is the participation of the judiciary. So is the provision of legal representation for the defence. Bottoms and McClean (1976) found 99 per cent of defendants in Crown Courts were professionally represented, 93 per cent on legal aid (p. 142). But the Crown Courts, where the ideology of justice is displayed in the form of judge, jury, and barrister for the defence deals with only 2 per cent of the business of the courts; 98 per cent of cases[16] are dealt with in the lower courts by summary justice and that is a different brand of justice altogether.

# 7 Two Tiers of Justice

The lower courts[1] are where most of the work of the criminal law is done—they are also where the characteristics of legality and justice are least in evidence.

To enter the lower courts is to be taken aback by the casualness and rapidity of the proceedings. The mental image of law carried into the courts is shattered by observation. The solemnity, the skills of advocacy, the objections, the slow, careful precision of evidence, the adversarial joust, none of these taken-for-granted legal images are in evidence. It seems to be another world from the legal system we have learned about in books, films, and television. The statistics tell the same story. Credibility in the ideology that the scales of justice are tipped to acquitting ten guilty men rather than convicting one innocent man is stretched to breaking point by the work of the lower courts. According to 1978 statistics the conviction rate in Scottish summary courts is 95 per cent, in English magistrates' courts 95 per cent for non-indictable offences and 93 per cent for indictable crimes. The combination of pleas and verdicts of guilt brought the total of convictions in the Sheffield magistrates' courts which Bottoms and McClean (1976) studied to 98.5 per cent (p. 106).

Magistrates' courts have, perhaps because of the blatancy of this contradiction, been the courts that have most attracted the scrutiny of sociology and social policy. Dell (1971) has shown that defendants remain 'silent in court' through fear or ignorance. Hetzler and Kanter (1974) have shown how the defendant stands in court at a situational disadvantage because of the symbolic layout of bench and dock. In particular, Carlen (1976) has demonstrated how the processing of defendants is achieved *situationally*, how the court team—magistrates, clerk of court, police, solicitors, probation officers—manages to obviate due process, suppress challenges, make the defendant a 'dummy player' by ruling him, whenever he speaks, out of time, out of place, out of order, even out of mind. All of these studies focus on the situation of participants, the use and avoidance of the rules. This study fully supports Carlen's description of the operation of summary justice but it changes the focus of analysis in three ways.

First it changes the stress from *use* of rules to the *rules* used, to the rules of procedure which actually define what is out of time, place or order, and to ironies not accomplished by the magistrate *in situ* but inherent in the structure of magistrates' justice. If the defendant, normally unrepresented, is the only one who does not know the rules, as every study of courts demonstrates, the cause must be traced beyond his ignorance, or the court team's games, to the paradox of a legal structure which requires knowledge of procedural propriety in making a case, and a legal policy which denies access to it.

Second, that paradox itself requires explanation too. A little delving into the historical development of magistrates' justice shows only too clearly that the high conviction rate in the face of all the safeguards for the defendant offered by legality is no mere situational accomplishment of the magistrates' court. Nor, indeed, is it accomplished by the High Court judges through the subtle qualifications, the ifs and buts of case law, maintaining the general rule but qualifying it for each particular case. It is the product of the heavy hand of legislation simply wiping out the rules as neither necessary nor relevant for the lower court at all.

The third concern is with Carlen's observation of the particular situational problems faced by the magistrates in presenting their work ideologically as justice. The higher courts are helped by 'rigid rules of ceremony' and 'traditional ceremonial costumes'. Magistrates have to 'produce a disciplined display of justice' *despite* the lack of solemnity and ceremony, lack of solicitors, and petty and marginal offences that characterise the lower courts (Carlen, 1976, p. 38). This chapter suggests that the lower courts in fact have no significant ideological function,[2] that the factors Carlen points to as situational problems for the production of magistrates' justice are the very factors which, by ideological sleight of hand, screen it from scrutiny, and indeed which accomplish the ultimate irony of protecting the ideology of justice while simultaneously denying it.

## SELF-DEFENCE

One of the crucial disadvantages pinpointed by all the studies of the accused in the lower courts is the fact that he is normally unrepresented. In Scotland there is now a duty solicitor scheme at all levels,[3] but duty stretches only to those in custody and stops at the point of plea—legal advice is available of right only to answer a charge, not to contest it. In England the defendant only exceptionally has a lawyer: Bottoms and McClean's Sheffield study found only 19 per cent represented throughout, compared with 99 per cent in the higher courts. The reason for this is simple enough: legal aid, though virtually a right in the higher courts, is not available in any but exceptional cases in the lower courts. Nor do the recommendations of the Royal Commission on Legal Services (1979) augur well for any significant change (p. 158).[4] The Widgery Committee on legal aid denied that a professional lawyer was normally necessary in the lower courts, implying that points of law, tracing and interviewing witnesses, or engaging in expert cross-examination were not normally involved. Yet the same report insisted that a professional lawyer *was* necessary for the higher courts:

> A layman, however competent, can rarely be relied on to possess the skill and knowledge necessary to put forward the defence effectively tried on *indictment* without the guidance of a lawyer. (Widgery, 1966, p. 79, my emphasis)

Were the structure and rules of procedure essentially different this distinction might be valid; differences there are, as we shall see, but not in the proof of a case. The trial, and with it the method of proof and the criteria of proof, remain exactly the same. There is the same adversarial structure, the same structure of proof by examination, cross-examination, the same requirement of direct witnesses to provide that proof, the same rules of evidence, *and the same requirement that the procedures be rigidly adhered to*. These are not laymen's courts but highly legalised proceedings.

The bench may be composed of lay magistrates, of course, though there is an increasing number of stipendiary magistrates in England, and in Scotland lay magistrates operate only on the fringes of criminal justice. But lay magistrates have clerks in England, assessors in Scotland, to keep the proceedings legally in check (both, according to Carlen's study, and this one, keen to stress legal technicalities exactly because that is their only justification for being there), while even the lay magistrates are themselves 'repeat players' with knowledge—or belief in their own knowledge—of the law. The prosecutor is *always* a professional lawyer in Scotland, while in England more and more police forces have prosecuting solicitors' departments to do the job professionally; and at worst the prosecution will be conducted by a policeman, a repeat player and a legal professional. All of this is at the state's expense, of course, which makes Widgery's conclusion on the provision of professional representation for the defence that 'there is a limit both to the number of practitioners who can provide legal assistance and to the funds that the state can reasonably be expected to make available' (Widgery, 1966, p. 14) appear something of a one-sided view. The provision of a prosecution is taken for granted; the provision of a defence is not. Yet the trial remains adversarial, and the legitim-ation of the adversary structure is exactly that it must be conducted by *equal* adversaries. To declare a professional defence unnecessary in this context is to put the accused into the ring as an amateur flyweight against professionals or heavyweights or both.

The plight of the unrepresented defendant in the magistrates' courts has often been put down to his lower-class background, and consequent lack of speech skills, articulateness, understanding. But as sociologists of education and speech have demonstrated, there is little essentially inarticulate about lower-class speech, and these same defendants recounting the same event of a Friday night in the pub as a story not as a case might do so with great aplomb. Nor is it necessarily fear (Dell, 1971) that prevents them getting their story across. Certainly surveys[5] have noted that more than half of defendants found the experience an ordeal, but that does not necessarily silence them. Fear might explain why so many people plead guilty: but all of those who pleaded *not* guilty in this study were prepared to tell their story to the magistrate. The problem was in fact that they were *too* prepared to do so to be mindful of courtroom procedures. Carlen describes how any challenges by the defendant to the actual administration and legitimacy of the law result in them being portrayed as 'out of place, out of time, out of mind, or out of order' (Carlen, 1976, p. 104). But the rules of time, place, and order are invoked much more routinely than this: they are not just emergency measures; but the very things which make a trial a trial, and the result is that the defendant is not only prevented from challenging the law but is routinely prevented from participat-ing in the trial.

The trial is organised into a quite definite order of events and at each stage different rules pertain:

(1) the defendant makes his plea;
(2) the prosecutor calls his witnesses—usually policemen—and examines them;
(3) the defendant can cross-examine each witness, immediately after the prosecution has examined him—at this stage the rule is that he can only ask questions of the witnesses not make statements on his own behalf;
(4) the defendant can, but only at this point and only if he moves from the dock to the witness box, make a statement;
(5) he is cross-examined in turn;
(6) if he has any witnesses he can examine them (again ask questions only) to elicit support for his story;
(7) they are cross-examined by the prosecutor;
(8) each party may sum up.

The defendant's first admissible opportunity to make a statement is at stage (4). But repeatedly he takes up the first invitation to speak, at stage (3), to deliver a statement to the magistrate, only to be rebuffed on procedural grounds. He is likewise interrupted or silenced with each witness until when it comes to his turn to enter the witness box (and often he starts his statement again in the dock only to be rebuffed or moved), he often rejects the chance or is quite taken aback to have a say. When he does speak he may well find his story interrupted and what seem to be crucial points excluded by the rules of evidence.

| | |
|---|---|
| Magistrate: | How do you know what they [the police] said to Pauline [co-accused]? |
| Accused: | She told us. |
| Magistrate: | That's hearsay. (Case 29) |

| | |
|---|---|
| Accused: | Sir I'd left before closing time to go to another pub. |
| Magistrate: | That's an alibi defence. You didn't intimate that.[In his summing up later he declared it inadmissible because no warning had been given]. (Case 1) |

In Case 27 the accused's defence depended on his having good reason to use a police phone:

| | |
|---|---|
| Magistrate: | Would you like to ask the officer any questions Mr McC? |

Accused: Do you know why I was on the phone?
Prosecutor: He can't answer that.

The unrepresented accused is not only denied access to knowledge of procedures but to the opportunity of being questioned. It may be easy to tell a long story in relaxed surroundings where the odd omission, carelessness or exaggeration in detail is irrelevant, but where all these things are likely to be picked up by an opponent, without an opportunity to redress them, it is easier to sustain a long detailed account via questions and answers, as indeed is sometimes made explicit in court. In Case 25 the prosecution witness was telling a long confused tale. The magistrate intervened to invoke the prosecutor into a more active role:

Magistrate: Do you think you could question him and get it a bit more clearly?

Defendants have the same problem. But with no lawyer representing them, there is no-one for the magistrate to call on to get the defence case clear. What is more, a lawyer with an eye to legal relevance will ask questions that make the account into a *case*,[6] something a layman might simply lack the knowledge to achieve.

Indeed a case is not made simply by presenting an account of one's own version of events. Proof in the adversary trial is achieved not just by building up the strong points in one's own case but by pointing out the weak points in one's opponent's. Proof has to be built up by countering the persuasive points in the opposing case or by destroying them, and given the nature of the evidence in minor offences, it is very often a necessity for the defendant not simply to remain silent or present an account that does not challenge police evidence, but actively to raise reasonable doubts in the prosecution case—remember the magistrate's conclusion: 'I see no reason to disbelieve the police' (Case 8). One way to raise such doubts is by cross-examination. Yet the Widgery Report (1966) sees professional cross-examination as rarely needed in summary cases (p. 47). This ignores the fact that in a good many cases this only denies professional cross-examination *of the prosecution case* since the prosecution will have a professional advocate to subject the *defendant* to professional cross-examination. Perhaps the implication is that the police do not need to be cross-examined because their version is correct. In any case that is the net result. Yet cross-examination is one of the essential weapons of the adversarial trial. With no cross-examination there is in a sense no trial and with no professional lawyer there tends to be no cross-examination, as observation in court demonstrates.

In order to be allowed to cross-examine his opponent just as in presenting his own story, the defendant must do so according to the rules and at the right stage of the procedure. But he is not necessarily told the procedure or the varying rules at each stage, and indeed he may not understand the distinctions in the rules between questions and statements, or be too intent on getting his story across to the magistrate at the first opportunity to abide by the formal rules of the court. His confusion of stages (3) and (4) of the trial's procedure not only tends to foil his attempt to present his case, it also foils the possibility of cross-examination taking place at all, so that the prosecution goes unchallenged. Take Case 1, for example, where four young men and one elderly man of no fixed abode were charged with breach of the peace. Only two were individually identified but they were all collectively identified as part of an aggressive crowd:

| | |
|---|---|
| Magistrate: | Would you like to ask any questions? |
| Accused 1: | [the elderly man]: All I said was 'what's happening?' |
| Magistrate: | [to policeman] Are you in any doubt that this man was committing the offence? |
| Policeman: | No |
| Accused 1: | I never opened my mouth except to ask what was happening. |
| Magistrate: | You can't deliver a peroration at this point. Have you [moving on to Accused 2] any questions? |

Accused 1 is left still on his feet looking baffled. Accused 2 shakes his head and the magistrate moves on to Accused 3.

| | |
|---|---|
| Accused 3: | What time was this? |
| Policeman: | 10.15 |
| Accused 3: | Sir, I'd left before closing time to go to another pub. |
| Magistrate: | That's an alibi defence. You didn't intimate that. Stay on your feet. Don't talk [to Accused 1 who |

was asking Accused 2 something in an agitated manner].

Accused 2:    [one of the two identified]: Sir, I had a beard that night.

Magistrate:   Ask him, don't tell me.

Accused 1, having had his response to the police story ruled out at the point of cross-examination with the first witness did not wait so long with the second one, but simply intervened to say that what was being said was not true. That attempt was ruled out too:

Magistrate:   I wish you wouldn't interrupt. It's bad manners.

Accused 1:    But I wasn't with them, I'm a stranger. They'll tell you if you ask them.

(This procedural heresy was of course ignored.)

Case 21 involved an Italian who could not speak English and therefore had an interpreter. When it came to stage (3) the assessor to the magistrate invited the accused to ask questions:

Assessor:     You'll realise it's difficult, but ask questions to the interpreter.

Accused:      No, I don't want to waste the court's time with language problems.

Magistrate and assessor both leapt in at this undermining of courtroom rhetoric:

Magistrate:   Oh we have all the time in the world.

Assessor:     The court's time is not wasted.

But the accused's 'question' was a statement; he simply stated what was incorrect in his view about the testimony. So it did not count; it did not have to be answered since it was not a question and since it was too early for a statement it lost him his turn. The magistrate, having gone overboard to invite him to speak, now simply stopped him: 'You'll get your chance later.'

Case 35 involved two teenage girls on a breach of the peace charge:

Magistrate:   At this time you ask the officer questions from the evidence he's given. Have you any questions?

| Accused: | We were just standing talking. |
| Magistrate: | [to policeman] She says they were just standing talking. Is this so? |
| Policeman: | No. |
| Magistrate: | That's the answer to your question. You may not like it but that's it. Move on to the next question. |
| Accused: | There's nothing else. |

Case 30 was the 'jumping on and off the pavement in a disorderly manner' case. The accused's 'cross-examination' consisted of no more than a series of statements of denial that he was part of the disorderly group, and the magistrate ultimately interrupted:

| Magistrate: | Are you satisfied, constable, that the boy was in the original group? |
| Policeman: | Yes. |
| Magistrate: | Right. Any other questions? |

Case 2 was about the theft of lead and involved 'verbals' which the accused denied:

| Policeman: | He said 'I took the chance because the sheriff comes to the house tomorrow and I need the money.' |
| Accused: | I said I got it from the coup [rubbish tip]. I didn't show him a sheriff's letter. |
| Magistrate: | Well he says he saw a letter that you produced. Next question. |

Case 29:

| Accused: | We were playing football and he came up and asked our name and about a TV. |
| Assessor: | [to policeman] Did you say this? |
| Policeman: | No. |
| Magistrate: | There's your answer. Any other questions? |

Case 5:

| Magistrate: | Any questions? |
| Accused: | I was only violent because I was being punched. |

| Magistrate: | Was he being assaulted? |
| Policeman: | No. We put him on the floor when he entered to await assistance. |
| Magistrate: | That's your answer. Any more questions? |

Case 25:

| Accused: | [to magistrate] Well all I can say is. . . |
| Magistrate: | It's him you ask the questions. |
| Accused: | No questions then. |

And so on. There are dozens of examples from the data—these are not peculiar cases but *typical* of the lower courts, as indeed the Lord Chancellor's office recognises in a series of lectures to magistrates:

> cross-examination and re-examination are difficult matters for unrepresented parties, and the help of the court is often necessary, just as it is necessary in most cases for the court to conduct the examination-in-chief. (1953, p. 38)

Several points are to be drawn from such examples. First, they demonstrate how the accused's ignorance of the procedures, inability to handle them, or indeed unmindfulness of them in his indignation or nervousness, leads to the magistrate simply silencing him. It is partly procedural nicety and grammatical pedantry that defines this as out of court because making a statement rather than asking a question is *not* cross-examination. It is also a matter of substance. For, and this is the second point, approaching an opposition witness with a direct denial and a clear statement of one's own case is *not* cross-examination in that it does not achieve the job cross-examination is fashioned for in the adversarial trial. It does not search out (or create the impression of) weakness in the opponent' evidence, or undermine the credibility of the witness. On the contrary it *underlines* the opposing case by giving the witness an easy opportunity to simply *deny* the defence. Professional cross-examination proceeds by quite different means, by indirect approaches, by a series of questions on apparently peripheral matters, with a crucial issue casually dropped in *en route*, by a series of questions leading the witness to an accusation which the witness cannot *logically* deny without discrediting his previous answers. The methods recommended by manuals on advocacy and used routinely by lawyers in court, are indirect and subtle. They may contradict the methods used in *non-legal* situations to establish truth but they *are* the stuff of cross-examination.

The unrepresented accused then all too often does *not* cross-examine; neither—and this is the third point—does the magistrate. An Act in 1903 for helping 'poor prisoners' to be legally represented, offered help only in exceptional circumstances on the grounds that 'where a prisoner was not defended by counsel his interests were safe in the hands of the presiding judge.' (Widgery, 1966 p. 2). And the lectures from the Lord Chancellor's Office already referred to remind the magistrate he may well need to help.

> If the defence when told he may cross-examine begins to make a statement and persists in doing so when told he must ask questions, the court will usually be able to turn his statements into questions on his behalf. . . . (1953, p. 38)

But as these examples from court observation show, putting cross-examination in the hands of the magistrate does not resolve the problem. This is not just because of the team games played out in court, nor indeed because of the personal characteristics, the impatience, hostility, or sarcasm of the magistrate, though they undoubtedly play a part, but precisely because the magistrate cannot cross-examine for the accused by turning his statements into questions. For a start it is too late: once the statement is put the surprise is lost. What is more, once the translated direct question is put it creates an impasse, a categorical denial, with nothing to pursue further. A competent professional advocate would never take this route. For the magistrate to do so does not therefore help the unrepresented accused conduct his cross-examination as a professional might, it simply ensures that his amateur cross-examination both terminates and fails. The magistrate's 'help' is therefore no substitute for defence advocacy. Nor could it be: that is not his role. The magistrate can, as all judges can, ask questions, but his role remains that of independant judge, he has no involvement in the preparation of cases and he may not take sides. And of course he does not know the defendant's version beforehand, so the questions he asks are necessarily coloured by the only version he has heard, the prosecution's. With the best will in the world he is not in the structural position to do the job of defence advocate.

Neither, for that matter, is the defendant. Indeed the un-represented defendant is truly in a dilemma. Without exercising the skills of the advocate or knowledge of the law he cannot participate in his trial, and there is no *defence*, but if he *does* demonstrate such skills he is caught in the double bind that he is not supposed to. Implicit in the notion of professional expertise is an unspoken closed shop which fosters the idea that only professionals *can* or *may* do the job. This indeed is an expectation promoted not only by experience of scores of baffled defendants but by authoritative sources, like the matter-of-fact observation in the Chancellor's lectures for magistrates, that: 'cross-examination and re-examination are difficult matters for unrepresented parties . . . (1953, p. 38). The result is that the accused who *does* cross-examine rather than make statements invites interruption and criticism, even though he is often pursuing only, if perhaps a little more agitatedly, the same lines that the professional would. In Case 6 the accused is invited to cross-examine for the second time with the quip: 'We don't want a breach of the peace here.' When one of the accused in Case 1 caught out the police witness on a detail of location, exactly the kind of detail advocates rub their hands over, he was interrupted by the magistrate (who after all had to decide his fate) with the comment: 'I wish you wouldn't be so aggressive—you're slightly offensive.' The same man had been cross-examining police witnesses as to identity with the trump card up his sleeve that he had a beard then and none now, yet this was not being noted when he was identified. Having tried to cross-examine the preceding two witnesses on this somewhat convolutedly but with enough grasp of the advocate's style to keep surprise on his side, he began on the third, only to be beaten to it by a direct question from the magistrate: 'How was he facially? Did he have a beard?' It is not at all unusual for prosecutors to conclude cross-examination of the accused with the suggestion that he is 'telling a pack of lies'. The same attack by an accused on the police is seen as insolent:

Accused:       [to police] I think you're a liar.
Assessor:      That's enough! (Case 29)

Ascertaining and trying to catch opponents out on details of time and place often take up a good deal of court time in represented cases but the unrepresented accused may not play the same game. In Case 9, one of the defendants tried to establish that the police could not, from their vantage point, have seen them 'touching cars' even if they were. The prosecutor in cross-examining him, reproved him:

Prosecutor:    So the story of touching cars is all lies.
Defendant:    Aye, that's all lies. I never touched it.
Prosecutor:    Why did you not ask the police that when they were here instead of about walls and curves in roads?

The magistrate had his say too:

Magistrate:    You're still a cocky young whippersnapper. When's your bubble going to burst? You're a very confident self-opinionated young man.

Dell may point to nerves as a problem for defendants but it would appear from such comments that confidence fares them little better. Defendants *may not* play the role of the confident punch-pulling advocate because it clashes not only with the incompetence and deference routinely demanded of the lower-class people who dominate the courts, but because it clashes with the role expected of the *defendant*. The defendant may be diffident, nervous, excited, contrite; he may not be confident, aggressive, cool, calculating, tricky—unless of course he is that rarety, an unrepresented middle-class defendant in the lower courts. The inherent characteristics of the competent defendant and the competent advocate make it structurally difficult to get away with playing both roles at once.

Defendants occasionally succeed in cross-examination, managing to suggest an alternative case without stepping over the threshold of the professional closed shop, succeed at least in the sense of winning judicial tolerance, if not of winning the case, as in Case 21. But this case ended as not proven on a technical lack in the prosecution case, not on the strength of the defence, while it was not only marked by exchange of smiles throughout between magistrate, assessor, and prosecutor but by comments among the court team at the end on how well the defendant had done, which rather suggested this was a phenomenon that was neither expected nor typical.

It is a normal technique of advocates to cross-examine on matters which appear to be peripheral as a way of catching the witness on a

crucial matter unawares, or indeed to make something significant of
a matter which may not seem so to the witness. Either way the
crucial elements are surprise and a continuity of flow in the
questioning, and a judge would be unlikely to intervene. Unrepresented defendants are not so readily accorded this privilege:

> Magistrate:    What's that got to do with it? Next question.
>                (Case 1)

Repetition, near-repetition, or persistence with a particular line,
normal enough advocacy styles, invite termination:

> Assessor:     I think you've covered that. I think we've got the
>               picture. (Case 21)

—though the assessor, having stopped this defendant, then went on
to ask questions on a new line only to tell the defendant when he
interrupted:

> Assessor:     You sit down—you've had your turn to cross-
>               examine. This is the court's turn.

Or the defendant's cross-examination may be ended by a simple
'Anything else?'—simple, but from *the* powerful court figure, be it
brusque, bored, or kindly, undeniably final. Magistrates exercise
much more control over defendants representing themselves than
over lawyers. Not only is there no professional etiquette to get in the
way but there is more of an immediate power relationship between
the defendant and the magistrate who holds the key to his fate than
between magistrate, or indeed judge, and lawyer.

It is not therefore just as simple as lawyers being able to do things
that laymen cannot. Even among defendants competent in the art of
self-defence it is harder for the unrepresented defendant to *get away
with* the same methods as a lawyer. Indeed to be too *au fait* with law,
procedure, and advocacy can mean inviting not just ridicule or
interruption but suspicion:

> Assessor:     Your vocabulary's very expressive, isn't it? You
>               know all about the powers. (Case 29) (General
>               Powers Act)

Or:

Magistrate:     It seems strange a young girl like you should
                know all this jargon if you've not been in trouble
                before. (Case 29)

The implication was made explicit when assessor, magistrate, and
prosecutor chatted together after the case:

Prosecutor:    They've been at it so often they know the score.

The accused is thus put in an absurd double bind—damned if he
is knowledgeable in the rules, competent in advocacy; damned if he
is not.

This analysis has examined the *situation* of the unrepresented
defendant in court, as others have, and it has set it in the fairly
obvious context of a structural paradox. The trial is predicated
upon professional knowledge, expertise, and adversarial advocacy,
but legal policy denies access to professional representation. Indeed
even status differentials in the lower courts can be explained in part
by legal policy. Not only are the occasional middle-class defendants
more likely to be articulate and competent, more likely than their
working-class counterparts, to be *expected* and *allowed* by court
personnel to be articulate and competent, and more likely to be able
to afford a lawyer themselves, but they are also more likely, if they
cannot, to be awarded legal aid. The Widgery Committee noted
that assessment of the need for a lawyer should take account of
variations in the consequences according to the social status of the
person involved:

> the seriousness of the consequences likely to result from loss of
> employment will also differ widely in different circumstances. A
> young labourer who loses his job in conditions of full employment
> will obviously not suffer to anything like the same extent as a
> middle aged black-coated worker who in the loss of his job,
> sacrifices career prospects, pension rights and may have the
> greatest difficulty in finding other comparable employment.
> (Widgery, 1966, p. 46)

Thus speaks the middle-aged black-coated judge. Likewise, though
the jeopardy of mere stigma resulting from a case is not of itself

enough to allow legal aid, it can be taken into account where it is, say, 'a *respectable* housewife charged with shoplifting' (my emphasis).

One policy implication of analysis at this level might seem clear enough: if legal policy denies the defendant—and particularly the working-class defendant—a lawyer, on the mistaken assumption he does not need one, and if empirical evidence shows he is at a disadvantage without one, then perhaps legal policy should remove the disadvantage by providing a lawyer. Leaving aside the financial consideration which undoubtedly motivated the Widgery Committee to minimise legal aid in the lower courts this seems simple. But the simplicity is in the analysis. The lack of a lawyer for the lower court defendant cannot be analysed simply as causing his problems nor indeed as *caused* by a paradox of policy and structure. That paradox is itself a symptom of a deeper structural and ideological distinction between higher and lower court justice, which implies that even with a lawyer the defendant in the lower court would have the odds weighted against him. To raise questions about the need for lawyers or the quality of their service before magistrates is to confuse the social roles of higher and lower courts. The lower courts are not there to stage grand ideological scenarios of proof by adversarial advocacy; they are simply in the business of summary justice.

## SUMMARY COURTS AND THE IDEOLOGY OF JUSTICE

Till the name was changed in 1952 the magistrates' courts were called courts of summary jurisdiction, as in Scotland they (and the Sheriff Courts operating without a jury) still are. What they offer is summary justice. Summary justice is characterised precisely by its *lack* of many of the attributes of the ideology of law, legality, and a fair trial. The *Oxford Dictionary* defines summary law as 'proceedings in a court of law carried out rapidly by the omission of certain formalities required by the common law'. The lack of representation is but one of many omissions. The judicial definition in Scots law is a procedure:

> without *induciae* and without indictment and further without any notice to the party of the names of the witnesses that are to be called against him and without the accused being represented by legal adviser unless he chooses to provide himself with one. (*Lamb* v. *Threshie*, 1892)

The judge might have added, without a record of the proceedings and of course without a jury. Summary justice is thus characterised legally not by positive attributes but by negative ones: it negates many of the procedures held to be necessary in the ideology of due process.

Controls are not very much in evidence either. Indeed till 1953 the accused could not even appeal against a magistrate's decision. Now he can appeal against sentence and have the case reheard at the Crown Court, so long as he does so within twenty-one days, and with the proviso that the sentence may be increased if he does appeal, something that is not possible for appeals from higher courts. He can also appeal against conviction on a point of law, though the method by which this is done in the lower courts, 'by case stated', is somewhat illogical as a method of control. Appeal against a magistrate is made by that magistrate stating the facts of the case to a higher court. There are no official records against which to check the magistrate's version. Nor does the defendant have an opportunity to give his own version of what occurred to cause him grievance. Thus in contradiction to the rest of the criminal justice system, the complaint is stated not by the complainant or independently by both complainant and defendant, but only by the person being complained against. Since all adversary legal procedure is geared to the idea that there are two contradictory versions of the facts in any dispute this is a total violation of its own assumptions. In law it is not stated like this of course. The appeal is presented as an appeal against the *prosecutor*: he is the 'respondent', and the magistrate is merely the independent judge. But it is of course the *magistrate*'s decision that is in question, and control would seem to be put in the hands of those whom it is supposed to control. Not surprisingly only 0.3 per cent of summary defendants on indictments, 0.4 per cent on non-indictable offences, appeal against conviction, and only a quarter of those succeed.

In all sorts of ways the formality of the higher court is abandoned. The indictments by which prosecutions are launched in the superior courts require absolute precision—even the size of the paper and margins are specified in the 1918 rules, but the 'information' which initiates the lower court prosecution has no set form, it need not even be written, though it usually is, and not all the elements of the offence need to be stated. Nor can any objection be raised to an 'information' on the grounds of defect of substance or form or because the evidence given at the trial varies from it (Arguile, 1969,

p. 55). Hence the administration of the lower courts is often
presented as less formal and legalistic than that of the higher courts.
But the 'informality' would seem to be rather one-sided: the
defendant's *role*, as this chapter has already shown, is still governed
by formal procedures, but the defendant's *rights* are greatly reduced.

If the lower courts seem to present a different world from the
image we carry in our heads of the higher courts then, it is hardly
surprising; in law that is exactly what they are. The law has created
two tiers of justice, one which is geared in its ideology and generality
at least to the structures of legality, and one which, quite simply and
explicitly, is not.


## STATE STRUGGLES AND THE TWO TIERS OF JUSTICE

The positive characteristics of summary justice are not legal so
much as economic and bureaucratic: summary justice is fast, easy
and cheap. The Scots manual, Renton and Brown (1972), notes 'the
facility and rapidity of summary process' (p. 184), while a
handbook for English law students observes that 'summary offences,
being both more numerous and less serious than indictable offences,
are tried by a simpler and cheaper method' (Price, 1979, p. 74).

But the appropriateness of simpler, cheaper procedure for minor
offences has not always been quite so taken for granted. In the early
days of the liberal democratic state after the 1688 Revolution the
judiciary viewed with considerable suspicion the operation of
summary justice, and convictions by JPs were constantly quashed
throughout the eighteenth century.[7] The grounds were often
technical, an inaccuracy in the form of the 'information' (the JPs
acting in the absence of an organised police force, on the word of
anonymous informers). Eighteenth-century justice was thus not
only marked by merciful pardons, as Hay (1975) has demonstrated,
nor indeed by technical acquittals by jurors, which have been put
down to the severity of the penalties, but by technical acquittals by
the judiciary of the higher courts. The reasoning displays not so
much a fetish for technicality, 'mere form or formality is not
required in these nor any other summary proceedings' (*R.* v.
*Chandler*, 1700), but as a deliberate policy of strict control over the
summary courts: 'a tight hand ought to be holden over these
summary convictions' (*R.* v. *Corden*, 1769). This may have been
because the theories from which democratic ideology emerged were

still recent enough for that ideology to be believed in and fervently upheld. The seventeenth-century common lawyers had, in their challenge to the monarchy, traced the pedigree of common law justice to no less than the Magna Carta and the famous dictum of Chapter 29 that

> No free man shall be taken and imprisoned or disseised of any free tenement or of his liberties or free customs or outlawed or exiled, or in any other way destroyed, nor will we go upon nor send upon him, *except by the lawful judgement of his peers* or by the law of the land[8]. (My emphasis)

Such rhetoric certainly jarred with the trial by 'a single justice of the peace in a private chamber upon the testimony of one witness' that summary justice offered:

> Everybody knows, that this being a penal law ought by equity and reason to be construed according to the letter of it and no further; and that this Act is penal is most plain, . . . and what is highly so, the defendant is put to a summary trial different from Magna Carta, for it is a fundamental privilege of Englishmen to be tried by jury, which privilege has been secured to us by our ancestors . . . (*R. v. Whistler*, 1699)

But summary jurisdiction was an affront to the common law judges not just because it violated the concept of justice celebrated in Magna Carta but by the fact that it was not a common law creation but was *statutory*. It had historically been introduced by the monarch, used oppressively by Henry II in particular, and thus, in a state now geared to keeping the monarchy in its place, must have had unfortunate connotations. But it was not done away with. On the contrary there were new interests involved. The new state was based on an idea of divided sovereignty, the separation of powers, but what that meant remained to be determined and there was still a battle to be fought out on the division of spoils. In the judiciary's technical acquittals on appeal from summary courts we may be witnessing a battle over the meaning of the separation of powers, with the judges claiming, on the basis of pre-parliamentary authority (hence the rhetoric of Magna Carta), exclusive rights over the operation of justice. Summary jurisdiction as a statutory creation offended this claim by being the prerogative of parliament.

The summary courts may thus have become one of the battlegrounds in the struggle over the form of the modern state; through such minutiae are the great battles of history fought out.

If this is correct, and it would require a deeper historical study than this to find out, it was a battle which the judges lost. By 1787 in the summary justice skirmish at least they were beginning to assume the role of the interpreters of parliament rather than its challengers and watchdogs, to define their role within the compass of parliamentary authority rather than as derived from a different tradition:

> As to the principle drawn from the old cases that the court will be astute in discovering defects in convictions before summary jurisdiction there seems to be no reason for it. Whether it was expedient that those jurisdictions should have been erected was a matter for the legislature; but as long as they exist we ought to go to all reasonable lengths to support their determinations. (*R. v. Thompson*, 1787)

In any case by the mid-nineteenth century in Acts 'to facilitate the performance of the duties of the Justices of the Peace' parliament had intervened decisively by simply removing the means by which convictions could be quashed. The judges had always insisted as the superior courts that detailed records were kept by the JPs. The more complete the more likely they were to disclose technical errors. Parliament now removed the need to keep a note of the evidence on which the conviction was based, and so made appeal and judicial control well nigh impossible. This move from excessive technicality might be seen as a simple—welcome—triumph for common sense over legalism. But for its full implications to be understood it should be set in the context of *why* the judges quashed summary convictions on technical grounds. One might speculate from the sparse evidence offered here that this represented not just mindless procedural fetishism but a means of upholding justice based on the ideology of the 'ancient rights of free men'. Technical acquittals may have defied common sense but they may also have been no more than a front for challenging not the case but the procedure *per se*. The irony is that the front itself, especially in the 'common sense' *par excellence* of Benthamism became an easy justification not for removing summary procedure but for removing the judges' control over it, by declaring technicalities irrelevant.

The Justices of the Peace lost their administrative role with the Municipal Corporation Act of 1835 but their judicial role began to expand. The 1847 Juvenile Offenders Act and the Summary Jurisdiction and Indictable Offences Act of 1848 allowed summary justices to deal with an increasing range of indictable offences. By the mid-nineteenth century more and more offences were being diverted from the higher courts to the summary courts (a process that continues one hundred years later in, for example, the James Report, 1975). Summary courts were also well established by the same period as courts freed from the due process of the common law. The apparent contradiction in the dictionary quotation cited earlier, 'proceedings in a court of law' which omit 'formalities required by the common law', may now be clearer. Courts of law can operate *without* what is required by law precisely because the courts in question are created by one strand of the state, parliament, and the rules by another, common law. The separation of powers thus provides the structural background for democratic ideology to operate despite its internal contradictions. The principles of one strand have remained as the dominant image of law and as the rhetoric of justice, but the existence of the other allows the legal system to deal with the vast majority of offenders in a way which flouts the principles of justice *legally*.

The short-circuiting of justice as traditionally defined required not just structural manoeuvring, however, but legitimation. Due process was and is ruled out of the lower courts as unnecessary on two grounds: first, both the offences and the penalties are too trivial; second, the issues and processes are such that the niceties of law and lawyers are irrelevant. The next sections analyse these legitimations to demonstrate their ideological nature, and their ideological accomplishments.

## THE IDEOLOGY OF TRIVIALITY

To read law books for information on the magistrates' courts is to come away with the clear impression that what goes on in them is overwhelmingly trivial. They deal with 'minor offences', 'everyday offences', 'the most ordinary cases', 'humdrum' events.[9] Legal academics even go so far—rare event—as indulging in jocularity. Coull and Merry's text gives the Scottish police courts, very much

the lowest tier of justice, seven lines, largely taken up with the fact
that they are empowered,

> inter alia to impose a fine of 50p for 'allowing a chimney to catch
> or be on fire' or a penalty of £2 for throwing 'any snowball, to the
> danger or annoyance' of any person. (Coull and Merry, 1971, pp.
> 25–6)

This dominant image of the triviality of the work of the lower
courts is shared by the press. The press benches in magistrates'
courts are rarely occupied. The column of offenders and penalties
that every local paper carries is the result of a phone call for results.
The proceedings themselves are of no interest, except perhaps to
provide this week's funny stories for the Diary column, institutionalised indeed in one Scottish paper[10] as 'little stories from
the police courts' where the comic antics and Glaswegian patter in
the dock of Big Bertha and Wee Annie are recounted for laughs.
And why not? Much of what happens in the court is—as Pat Carlen
demonstrates—funny or pathetic or absurd, and so very trivial, too
trivial to attract any serious attention from the press.

Nor indeed from the public: so rare is it for a member of the public
to attend summary courts that the public benches are often used as a
waiting room for the morning's batch of defendants, from which
they can observe their predecessors' fate and shuffle along to each
newly vacated space till their turn comes for the dock. To go to these
courts as a member of the public is to become an object of curiosity;
to sit there taking notes is to invite paroxysms of paranoia. I have
been asked by one police officer on duty if I was 'from one of those
radical papers' by another if I was 'just here to practise your
shorthand, dear?' I've been called before the bench to explain
myself, had a policeman sent by the magistrate to ask me what I was
doing there, been advised not to take notes by a policeman on duty,
told by another that taking notes was illegal, and instructed by yet
another, not to note down an altercation between an assessor (the
legal adviser to a lay magistrate in Scotland) and a solicitor—it
wasn't 'done'. The 'public' in the lower court is an unusual
phenomenon, and the purveyors of magistrates' justice are somewhat sensitive to anyone seeing their particular brand of justice
being done. More than that, some were just genuinely concerned
that I should be wasting my time at the lower courts when I could be
watching 'juicy cases' and 'real judges' elsewhere. *Their* assumption

was that the work of *their* court was too trivial to be of interest. So the image of triviality that pervades the lowest ranks of criminal justice has the consequence of removing yet another requisite of due process: that the administration of justice should be public. One of the objections of the eighteenth-century judges to summary justice was that it was 'in a private chamber' behind closed doors. The doors were opened in 1848 but the dominant image of triviality helps ensure that the public benches remain empty. It is not just the offences that are deemed trivial—drunkenness, swearing, petty theft (a report by the Chief Constable for Glasgow (1975) noted that 47 per cent of all thefts were of goods valued under £10)—but the penalties, and the triviality of the penalties may help in particular to explain public apathy. Not only is it difficult to work up a moral panic over someone 'jumping on and off the pavement in a disorderly manner', taking lead worth 20p from a rubbish tip or touching cars, but the life-and-death decision of Hay's eighteenth-century courts is missing. The salacious fascination of whether the scales would tip to the gallows or mercy can hardly be matched by crimes whose *maximum* penalties are six months in prison or a fine of £1000.

More specifically, it is the relative triviality of the *penalties* that provides the crucial legitimations in law for the lack of due process in summary justice. Due process of law is required in the ideology of democratic justice before a person's liberty may be interfered with. The reasoning which legitimises reducing due process in the lowest courts is based on this premise, but with a refinement. 'Liberty' ceases to be an absolute and becomes subject to a measuring rod. The limited penalties available to magistrates means they can interfere less with one's liberty than the higher courts, so defendants in these courts need less due process. The less one's liberty is at risk the less one needs protection. This is perhaps most explicitly stated in the criteria for awarding legal aid. One important condition is where the defendant is 'in real jeopardy of losing his liberty or livelihood or suffering imprisonment' (Widgery, 1966; Royal Commission on Legal Services, 1979, p. 158).

More generally this is in many ways a strange argument. 'Trivial' offences after all still involve state intervention in the citizen's liberty. Indeed if the same due process is not to be awarded to all defendants, it might seem a bit illogical to minimise the legal rights for those who have allegedly infringed least on law and order and maximise them for those who have infringed most. Perhaps it is just that the more unusual the crime, and the larger the penalty, the more public interest is likely to be aroused and the more justice will be willy-nilly on display. The more criminality in the offence, the more legality in the proceedings might be an odd equation. The more *publicity*, the more legality, is in ideological terms, perfectly understandable. Publicity is not an issue that need trouble lower court justice, closeted from the public eye by its own triviality—or more accurately, by its own ideology of triviality. Triviality is not just a description but an interpretation, an assessment, and the work of the lower courts could be viewed quite differently.

For a start, offences and penalties may seem trivial from the outside but far from trivial from the perspective of the accused—unless they have become so only through the folk memory[11] of the lower-class people who pass through the court, to whom police and law have become enemies, and prosecution for trivial offences a risk of everyday life. The James Report rejected the perspective of the defendant as a way of categorising which offences and penalties were serious and which were not, on grounds which stressed its significance but also its bureaucratic inconvenience: 'It would be impracticable . . . since that importance varies according to his character and position in society' (James Report, 1975, p. 20), though the same reasoning is used in the Widgery Report to do the opposite; that is, to use the defendant's perspective, *as it varies according to his social status*, to justify discriminating in favour of the middle class in the award of legal aid.[12] Thus the very people who are *expected* rightly or wrongly to be more competent in handling both authorities and formal, verbal situations, are the ones who are also made the exceptions who need additional professional help. One is tempted to conclude from such careful exceptions that the ideology of triviality may ultimately derive less from the triviality of the offences or the penalties but from the triviality in authoritative eyes of *the people*, the lower class and lower still, the unemployed, homeless, feeble, who provide the fodder for the lower courts—an implication indeed which is supported by the fact that the only time the lower courts become news is when, for example, Mark Phillips is charged with speeding.

Nor is it just a question of perspective but a question of focus. There is an inherent paradox in the very idea of prosecuting trivial offences. They are too trivial to interest the public but not too trivial for the state to prosecute in the name of the public; too trivial to merit due process of law but not too trivial for the intervention of the law. The ideology of triviality focuses on the offences and penalties, not on the question of prosecution itself. It is these trivial offences after all which, as we have seen in Chapter 3, are: first, most open to the direct intervention of the state in the sense that the police are the *only complainants*; second, most open to the imposition of a criminal label on 'marginal' behaviour; and third, most open—because their content is so open—to *post hoc* law-making. In short, it is exactly in the area of minor offences that the operation of the law, in terms of democratic justice, becomes most suspect. If the behaviour involved in the offence is not intrinsically interesting, perhaps, as the eighteenth-century judges felt, the law's processing of that behaviour into an offence is. But contemporary official discourse is more concerned with the quantity of crime than the quality of justice, and the lower courts remain something to be laughed at or yawned over for the pettiness of their crimes, not watched with care for the marginality of their legality.

## LEGAL RELEVANCE

The second justification for reducing the strictures of due process— a view indeed taken for granted by socio-legal writers like Mungham and Thomas (1979)—is that the offences dealt with in the lower courts do not involve much law or require much legal expertise or advocacy. They can therefore be safely left to be dealt with by laymen[13]—by lay magistrates and by the defendants themselves, with lawyers seen as normally unnecessary in the lower courts. According to the Widgery Report, legal aid is rarely necessary for summary offences since: 'The large majority of cases are straightforward and the facts are uncomplicated and clear-cut' (Widgery Report, 1966, p. 47).

But this view of the lower court is inaccurate in two ways. First, empirical study, as already demonstrated, shows that the lower courts are permeated by legalistic and professional consciousness. Second, it is logically confused—it confuses cause and effect. The reasoning in the Widgery Report, and Mungham and Thomas' essay, verges on tautology. It might just as readily be argued that minor offences are characterised by simple facts and straightforward cases because lawyers are so rarely involved. The 'case' is a construct from an event, not a reproduction of it. The construction of a case as straightforward or as involving points of law is very much the product of the advocate's trade. Case law, after all, develops exactly because advocates present cases which draw subtle distinctions and shades of meaning; in short, complicate the simple, in arguing for the treatment of the case in hand as different from previous cases. What is more, case law and the development of complicated and difficult legal issues in specific types of offence and case, is predicated largely on the right to appeal on points of law, and both the nature of the appeal procedure in the lower courts and the lack of lawyers to formulate an appeal on a point of law, means that there is little opportunity to develop difficult and complex case law on minor offences. It is not in the nature of drunkenness, breach of the peace or petty theft to be less susceptible than fraud, burglary or murder to complex legal argument; it is rather in the nature of the procedure by which they are tried. Indeed the James Report implicitly recognises this when it notes that: 'trial on indictment takes longer than summary trial even for a case of similar gravity and complexity' (James Report, 1975, p. 13). And of course the eighteenth-century judges found plenty of legal niceties in the work of the summary courts, until they were explicitly deprived of the means to intervene. The comment in the Lords debate on the 1952 Magistrates' Act that the high courts were not aware of what went on in the magistrates' courts because: 'in the nature of things their professional skill has led them into the higher reaches of the law rather than the more humdrum reaches of the magistrates' courts'. (Hansard, 1952, p. 1223) ignores the use to which professional skill was put historically, and the legislative axe that ended it. The 'straightforward cases' of the lower courts are themselves legal constructions.

The same is true of the 'simple facts'. The facts of a case—a case of any sort—are not *all* the elements of the event, but the information allowed in by the rules, presented by the witnesses, and surviving the credibility test of cross-examination. The facts of summary cases may not be simple because of the nature of the offence but because of the lack of professional expertise in manipulation of the rules, persuasive presentation of one's own case and destructive cross-examination of the other side's. It is not that complex facts need lawyers, but that lawyers can make 'facts' complex. That is exactly their trade.

Or the facts may be 'simple' not because of the nature of the behaviour in the offence but because of the nature of the *definition* of the offence. As Chapter 3 suggested the openness of the legal definition of what constitutes an offence, along with the fact that these offences are normally the result not of citizens' reports but of police-accused encounters—with only the accused's word against the policeman's constituting the case—means that it is extremely difficult to establish a defence. In short, the facts are simple only because they are legally so difficult for the defendant to contest.

Indeed it might be suggested that the openness of the laws defining summary offences argues not for less legal expertise but for more. If the police can legally define almost anything as an offence, then the facts cannot be in dispute and the only way to establish a defence is on a point of law. Remember Case 30, the 'jumping on and off a pavement in a disorderly manner' case. One reaction to being charged for that, even if one *was* doing it, might be total disbelief and a defence on the basis of it being absurd to be taken to court for such behaviour at all. But that of course is not a legal defence, just a cut-and-dried admission of guilt. The accused in this case, the only one of the group charged who pleaded not guilty, defended himself by saying he was not doing anything disorderly, that indeed he had just crossed the road to talk to the group collected at the tenement entrance, and that he didn't run away because he 'didn't expect to be lifted'. That was his mistake. The prosecution even noted in his concluding speech that: 'he may think he wasn't misbehaving as much as the others *but he stayed with them*'. And that was all that was necessary in law.[14] There was therefore no legal defence in denying his behaviour was offensive, not only because that was difficult to maintain against two policemen but because in law it was irrelevant. A relevant defence would have to take on the meaning of the law; for example, contending that to be 'part of a disorderly crowd' requires not just one's presence but active participation. But that would be a point of law: it would require a more sophisticated knowledge of law and legal reasoning than this layman had, and of course, as we've already seen, might require presentation by a lawyer to be given a hearing at all. The irony is then that because of the openness of the law on minor offences, kept open because there is so little case law to specify meaning, the best route to a defence is to challenge on a point of law. This of course could *establish* that missing case law, but it cannot be readily done because no need for lawyers is perceived, and the means to raise a point of law are denied. The image of the lower courts as not needing lawyers, which justifies not providing lawyers, is itself a *product* of their absence. The defendant is thus caught up in the vicious circle that lies behind the image of 'simple facts' and 'straightforward cases'.

But, and this is why situational analysis needs to be set in its deeper structural context, providing lawyers would not necessarily make any difference: the ideologies of non-law and triviality pervade the origins and structure of the lower courts and so pervade the attitudes of those who work in them. Remember the police official who helpfully suggested I go to the higher courts for 'juicy cases' and 'real judges'. And lawyers themselves often operate with a different style in the lower courts. Indeed they are different lawyers. The non-law ideology has its structural expression in the idea that only barristers can act in the higher courts but only solicitors can usually be provided on legal aid in the lower courts. This is not to suggest insidious comparisons between the skills of solicitors and barristers, but merely to indicate that whatever the personal attitudes or competence of the solicitors who do appear in the lower courts the standard of advocacy *required* is pre-set as second class. Likewise there is a structural expectation that lower courts do not need cases that are well prepared, or indeed prepared beforehand at all, by either side. With no committal proceedings the defence has no advance warning of the prosecution case it will have to face anyway, while Arguile's book on criminal procedure notes that if a matter arises in the defence evidence that takes the prosecution by surprise he may call evidence in rebuttal of it *afterwards*:

> This is permitted because summary trials usually owe very little to advance preparation of the case, and the prosecution is therefore more likely to be surprised by unexpected defences. (Arguile, 1969, p. 164)

This is certainly borne out by observation, as indeed is the idea that lawyers consider lower court cases too trivial, or too simple, to be worth much bother. In Case 17 two brothers charged with breach of the peace while on business in Scotland had pleaded not guilty and come all the way from London to stand trial. They had hired a solicitor and provided him with the details of their case. He did not turn up. The brothers were adamant they would not continue without a solicitor, though they earned themselves a few rude comments as a result. A solicitor from the same firm who

happened to be in the building agreed to step in, and began to find
out about the case there in court, suppressing one of his new clients'
indignation at these proceedings with the reprimand that *he* should
have reminded the solicitor of the date and venue of the trial: 'I'd
have thought someone who knows as much about the law as you
would know that.' And he added the ultimate put-down that in any
case: 'Breach of the peace isn't a serious charge.'

There were lawyers who operated as advocates, prepared
efficient cases, organised witnesses. They tended to be young, one
was a woman, all were patronised by the court officials as new to the
game and trying a bit too hard. *The reaction of the court* suggested they
were not typical. There was even one who launched into
technicalities, refusing to let his client stand trial because he had
turned up on the due date given him and the court had not tried
him—the clerk had got the date wrong and made it a Sunday (Case
18). He was, in a tired tone, given a new date: such technical details
are expressly ruled out as unimportant in the lower courts. Another,
representing the middle-class owner of a pub on a strict liability
licensing charge, even raised a point of law, cited precedents and got
the court very excited. This was such an unusual occurrence they
had to adjourn to find the relevant books (Case 14). There were
others, however, who simply left their clients as dumbfounded as the
defendant in Case 8. McD. had been so adamant he was innocent
that he and his mother had hired a lawyer at their own expense.
And in their view, 'it was the easiest £30 I ever saw anyone earning'.
There *was* a witness, a stranger, who, according to the defendant,
had in fact been committing the offence, and had been prepared to
give evidence that McD. had arrived *after* the event. He had
pleaded guilty, but recognised McD. was not and gave a statement
to that effect to the lawyer. Summoning him was left to the
defendant's mother. Neither she not the witness had a phone. She
sent her seven-year-old son with a note. The witness's father took it
at the door. She never knew if the witness himself received it. He
certainly did not turn up. In court, the defence lawyer merely noted
'I had hoped to have some supporting evidence but unfortunately
for one reason or another it is not available.' The magistrate, not
surprisingly, saw 'no reason why I should doubt the evidence given
by the policeman'. And the family even less surprisingly concluded:
'People like us don't have rights.'

Comments on the lawyers in my observed cases must necessarily
be scant and may be unrepresentative. This was a qualitative study

of a relatively small number of cases and the number of lawyers was in the nature of things—and particularly in the nature of legal aid— few. There are other snippets of information that may lend support though: for example, Darbyshire's study of justices' clerks and her description of the courts as dominated by a handful of solicitors usually engaged on several cases at once, and always holding things up, or by inexperienced young barristers who 'hadn't a clue'. She assessed the level of advocacy she observed in action as generally 'mediocre' and 'appalling' with little legal argument, and with (to her) obvious defences either not put at all or put as mitigation which if accepted would amount to a complete defence (Darbyshire, 1978, p. 239). There is also the criticism of the level of advocacy in the magistrates' courts made to the Royal Commission on Legal Services by the Association of Magisterial Officers. My concern, however, is less with assessing the level of performance and attitude of lawyers *per se* than with teasing out what that demonstrates about the professional lawyer's ideology of the lower courts. On that score, the reply by the Law Association is as telling as the criticism. First the magisterial officers are themselves derided for both their menial status and their lack of law since they 'for the most part probably entirely lack legal qualification and were formerly called the National Association of Justices' Clerks' Assistants'. Then the offenders and offences and work of the court in general is discussed as 'relative trivia' and 'the dross of the criminal courts'. The suggestion by the officers that such offenders and offences need specialists to deal with them is noted as showing 'how divorced from reality their comments must be' and as 'the best indication of the unreliability of this evidence and the lack of thought which appears to have preceded it' *(The Times*, 23 August 1977). What these comments suggest is that the profession too is imbued with the dominant images of the lower courts as neither serious enough nor legally relevant enough to need lawyers. To simply prescribe lawyers on tap for the lower courts as a solution to the defendant's dilemma is thus to ignore the much more fundamental structural and ideological realities which lie behind the courtroom situation.

## THE ACCOMPLISHMENTS

These images of the court are not just ideological accomplishments; they also accomplish ideological functions themselves. Carlen points to the marginality of the offences, the lack of ceremony and lack of lawyers in the lower courts, as a problem for the magistrate in presenting the court's work as justice (Carlen, 1976, p. 38). But the situational problem is in fact resolved structurally. The very same factors are transformed into images of the court as trivial and non-legal: and the effect of those images is that the court never actually has to account for its work anyway. The magistrate may have an existential problem in portraying his work as justice but he rarely has a social problem. For the magistrates' court is a theatre without an audience.

Legal policy has established two tiers of justice. One, the higher courts, is for public consumption, the arena where the ideology of justice is put on display. The other, the lower courts, deliberately structured in defiance of the ideology of justice, is concerned less with subtle ideological messages than with direct control. The latter is closeted from the public eye by the ideology of triviality, so the higher courts alone feed into the public image of what the law does and how it operates. But the higher courts deal with only 2 per cent of the cases that pass through the criminal courts. Almost all criminal law is acted out in the lower courts *without* traditional due process. But of course what happens in the lower courts is not only trivial, it is not really law. So the position is turned on its head. The 98 per cent becomes the exception to the rule of 'real law' and the working of the law comes to be *typified not* by its routine nature, but by its *atypical*, indeed *exceptional*, High Court form. Between them the ideologies of triviality and legal irrelevance accomplish the remarkable feats of defining 98 per cent of court cases not only as exceptions to the rule of due process, but also as of no public interest whatsoever. The traditional ideology of justice can thus survive the contradiction that the summary courts blatantly ignore it every day—and that they were set up precisely for that purpose.

# 8 Conclusion and Implications

## UNDERSTANDING LAW ENFORCEMENT: A NEW PERSPECTIVE

This study set out to analyse the role of legal forms, powers, privileges, limitations, and rulings on the process of constructing conviction in court—conviction in both the subjective sense of how a judge or jury comes to be convinced beyond reasonable doubt of its verdict, and in the legal sense of a finding of guilt; for that, statistically, is the likely outcome of a foray into the criminal courts. The problem for the sociologist is how that is possible when all the rhetoric of the democratic ideology of justice proclaims that in the battle between the state and the accused the system is heavily biased in favour of the latter. By examining the law not just in terms of the general principles of its own ideology, but in terms of the details of its specific structures, procedures, and decisions, this analysis has tried to show that the law governing the production, preparation, and presentation of evidence does not live up to its own rhetoric.

The rhetoric of justice requires incriminating evidence as the basis for arrest and search; the law allows arrest and search in order to establish it. Justice requires that no-one need incriminate himself; the law refuses to control the production of confessions and allows silence as a factor in proving guilt. Justice requires equality; the law discriminates against the homeless, the jobless, the disreputable. Justice requires each case be judged on its own facts; the law makes previous convictions grounds for defining behaviour as an offence and evidence against the accused. Justice places the burden of proof on the prosecutor; the law qualifies the standard and method of proof required and offers the prosecutor opportunities for making a case which the accused is denied. Justice proclaims the right to trial by one's peers; the legal system ensures that 91 per cent of all defendants plead guilty, and of the rest most are tried without a jury.

If, then, the process of conviction is easier than the rhetoric of justice would have us expect—and easier still the lower the status of the defendant—it is hardly surprising. A wide range of prosecution evidence can be legally produced and presented, despite the rhetoric of a system geared overwhelmingly to safeguards for the accused, precisely because legal structure, legal procedure, legal rulings, *not* legal rhetoric, govern the legitimate practice of criminal justice, and there is quite simply a distinct gap between the substance and the ideology of the law.

This conclusion has two direct and immediate implications. First it places the contemporary policy debate over law and order in a new light. The police demand for more powers, for the removal of the hamstrings of the right to silence, the limitations on arrest and search—and indeed the civil liberties camp's agitated response that the legal checks of British justice must be upheld—begin to appear rather odd. *Both* sides of the debate are framed in terms of the ideology of civil rights, not in terms of the realities of legal procedure and case law which, as I hope this analysis has amply shown, have all too often already given the police and prosecution the very powers they are demanding. The law does not need reform to remove hamstrings on the police: they exist largely in the unrealised rhetoric.

Second, more theoretically, this analysis has implications for the explanation of law-enforcement and its outcomes. A whole range of excellent sociological studies has pointed out situational, informal, non-legal factors in police–citizen encounters and courtroom interaction to explain *who* is arrested or convicted, and to explain why the system so often seems *in practice* to be weighted against the accused. Their answer lies essentially in the complex nature of social interaction and motivation; in the fact that people do not merely administer the law but act upon and alter it as they do so. This study offers a supplementary perspective, making the law rather than the activities of its administrators problematic. The conclusion is quite different. Given the formal procedures and rules of the law and the *structure* of arrest, investigation, plea and trial, one could not—even if human beings acted entirely as legal automatons—expect the outcomes to be other than they are. If the practice of criminal justice does not live up to its rhetoric one should not look only to the interactions and negotiations of those who put the law into practice ut to the law itself. One should not look just to how the rhetoric of justice is subverted intentionally or otherwise by policemen bending the rules, by lawyers negotiating adversariness out of existence, by out-of-touch judges or biased magistrates: one must also look at how it is subverted *in the law*. Police and court officials need not abuse the law to subvert the principles of justice; they need only use it. Deviation from the rhetoric of legality and justice is institutionalised in the law itself.

Coming back to Packer's two polar types for describing law-enforcement, due process and crime control, empirical analysis of the process reveals them as a false distinction. The law on criminal procedure in its current form does not so much set a standard of legality from which the police deviate as provide a licence to ignore it. If we bring due process down from the dizzy heights of abstraction and subject it to empirical scrutiny, the conclusion must be that due process is *for* crime control.

This perspective offers quite a different ideological gloss on the nature of criminal justice and a shift of focus for its study. Focusing on the subversion of justice by its petty administrators, on the gap between the law in the books and the law in action, in effect whitewashes the law itself and those who make it. Front-men like the police become the 'fall guys' of the legal system taking the blame for any injustices in the operation of the law, both in theory (in the assumption like Skolnick's that they break the rules) and indeed, in the law. The law holds the individual policeman personally responsible for contraventions of legality that are successfully sued, while at the same time refusing to make clear until after the event exactly what the police are supposed to do. It is no coincidence that the police themselves asked for the original Judges' Rules. Shifting the focus to the substance of law places responsibility for the operation of criminal justice—and the need for the spotlight of study—squarely on the judicial and political élites who make it.

Tracing a gap between the rhetoric of justice and the substance and structure of law is not, however, just the end of a piece of indignant exposé research (Taylor, Walton, and Young 1975, p. 29). It opens up a whole complex of further issues. If the contradictions between rhetoric and practice in law-enforcement cannot simply be explained away as the unintended consequences of the action of petty officials, then we are faced with contradictions within the core of the state between the ideology and substance of the law. Why does such institutionalised deviation occur? How is the ideological gap managed? What implications does it have for the idea of the rule of law? Though these are major issues which each require a full-scale study in themselves, the sections that follow offer some speculative beginnings.

## RHETORIC AND LAW: WHY THE GAP?

It is too simple to discuss the gap between the rhetoric of justice and the substance of law as unproblematic, as the inevitable and self-evident consequence of a class society in which the rhetoric of justice is necessarily mere illusion. Some more sophisticated analyses have been suggested. Hall and his colleagues (1978) have tried to offer a materialist explanation of a particular move in the 1970s to a more repressive crime-control oriented use of law and steady erosion of civil liberties by relating it to a crisis in the hegemony of the bourgeois state, and that in turn to economic crisis. At another level of contextual analysis a series of sociologists,[1] including indeed Hall *et al.*, have demonstrated how a moral panic and campaign for the repression of a particular social problem—mugging, football hooliganism, drugs, mods and rockers—can lead to more crime-control oriented judicial decisions, and so help explain why particular swings in the orientation of law to or away from the rhetoric of justice take place. It might also be possible, however, that a tendency one way or the other exists in the law itself. From examining the legal structure it would seem that there are also forces *within* the law which might well lead *routinely*—when there are no moral panics in either direction—to a development of case law that favours crime control rather than due process.

Case law and judicial discretion could as readily be used—and indeed have been—to condemn police practices as to condone them. But case law emanates, to state the obvious, from particular trials. There is no public interest law in Britain, no way in which a point of law can be brought to court as an abstract issue of public concern. A point of law can only be clarified in the context of a dispute in a real case, either directly at a High Court trial from the decision taken by the judge on a dispute over a point of law, or indirectly via appeal from the trial court to the Court of Appeal or House of Lords. Locating the dispute over law in the facts of a concrete case might well, despite the distinction drawn in legal theory between issues of fact and issues of law, mean that the facts of

the case affect the finding in law by providing the context in which
the decision has to be made. What this whole study has suggested is
that that context, if the point of law is being raised in the course of a
trial, is one in which the accused is likely to look guilty. If it is being
raised on appeal, then he will already have been *found* guilty since, in
the main, only defendants can appeal, and only defendants with a
grievance—that is, those who have been convicted.[2] What is more,
because re-trials of fact, or the introduction of new evidence, are
rarely allowed on appeal, that defendant's case is often of necessity
based on technicality rather than equity, on the means by which the
evidence was acquired rather than the misleading or inaccurate
nature of the evidence itself. Judges making case law on appeal are
thus faced in effect with a guilty defendant trying to argue his way
out of his due deserts through legal technicalities. Who would blame
them for closing the escape route by removing the technicality, by
seeing rights as loopholes that should in the name of justice be
removed? If these hypotheses are correct, one can readily see why in
particular cases judges may be likely to decide against the accused.

The problem is that judges are exercising a dual function in
reaching their decision. They must not just ensure that justice is
done in the sense of the accused getting his deserts; they must also
ensure that the technical checks on *how* criminal justice is executed
are upheld. They must not just uphold the substantive criminal law
but the procedures of legality. They must think not only of the
apparently guilty man before them but of the protection of the
innocent in the future. But this duality of function sets up an
impossible contradiction. The decision is a finding for *either* one
party *or* the other. It has *either* to declare the methods illegitimate,
the evidence inadmissible and quash the defendant's conviction, *or*
uphold the conviction, but in doing so, inevitably legitimise the
questionable methods—inevitably because of a second duality in
the function of decisions. The judicial decision does not just resolve
the particular case but sets a precedent for future cases. Provisos in
civil rights introduced in the context of a particular case become
abstracted and available for argument in all cases. Rejecting a
technical defence may be quite understandable in the context of
the black-and-white cases constructed through advocacy and
procedure, but with every rejection of a technical defence case
comes an extension of police and prosecution powers. Civil liberties
cease to be legal rights and the control of crime is safeguarded at the
expense of legality.[3]

In short, from the structure of trial and appeal, and from the functional dualities in the judicial decision—deciding on both the individual case and the law; upholding both substantive and procedural law—one can plausibly hypothesise a structural trend in case law towards crime control and away from due process. While contextual analysis is obviously vital, the legal system itself may also help explain why substantive law might routinely be upheld at the expense of procedural law and the rights of the rhetoric of justice gradually whittled away.

## MANAGING THE IDEOLOGICAL GAP

The gap between the rhetoric of justice and the substance and structure of law raises not only 'why' questions but 'how' questions. How is it possible for the law to deviate from the rhetoric, and how does the rhetoric survive the deviation? Much has been made of the tension between due process and crime control but the law seems to achieve crime control while keeping the ideology of due process in play;[4] it seems to achieve in some measure at least the impossible task of maintaining two contradictory ideas at once. How are the ideological gap and the ideological contradictions managed?

Part of the answer lies in the mystique and inaccessibility which protects the detail of law from the mass of people. It is the rhetoric rather than the law that is public knowledge. Indeed one can observe defendants losing their case precisely because they are arguing it on the basis of the rhetoric rather than the law. One needs a knowledge of both law and rhetoric before the gap between them becomes evident. What is more, a good deal of what occurs in the courts, as argued in Chapter 5, may appear to fit the rhetoric of justice only because the organisation of the facts into not only black-and-white cases but into black-and-white cases that are likely to persuade ordinary people of guilt has taken place *out* of the public eye. The ideological shutters around the magistrates' courts (Chapter 7) and the difficulties attached even to getting leave to appeal, have the same effect. The division of the process into public and private faces helps in itself to maintain the ideology.

Part of the answer lies too in the techniques of judicial reasoning. Judges deciding a point of law routinely reiterate the rhetoric in resounding prose, yet decide the case in such a way that the rhetoric is, for this individual, effectively denied. Throughout we have seen examples of how this apparent contradiction is calmly and routinely accomplished. Judges may draw literal distinctions which re-iterate the principle but make it simultaneously irrelevant or indeed uphold the principle but give such specific reasons that it cannot be generalised, as in *Lawrie* v. *Muir* or *H. M. Adv.* v. *Aitken*.[5] They may avoid the applicability of the rhetoric by redefining the situation in such a way that it is no longer covered by the principle; for example, creating the limbo of the 'suspect' who was thus not protected by the rhetoric or law on arrest and interrogation.[6] They may uphold the rhetoric by expressing dissatisfaction with the questionable means used to acquire evidence, but simultaneously allow that evidence to be used to convict on other grounds, maintaining that the trial judge has discretion in such matters as to precisely how it should be applied as in the *R.* v. *Lemsatef* case,[7] or deciding—on no rational empirical grounds at all—that the conviction by the jury did not depend on that piece of evidence anyway. All kinds of techniques of reasoning allow the rhetoric to be both eulogised and denied.

But structural factors also provide some of the means of bridging the ideological gap. The doctrine of the separation of powers provides a multi-headed state and with it the potential to extol the rhetoric in one sector and deny it in another. Statutes may provide rights in general terms—the 1887 Act, for example, made provision for a defendant to consult a solicitor—only to have the judges refine the right out of existence.[8] The rhetoric lives on in the statute but is routinely negated in the courts by judicial reasoning.

Beneath judicial reasoning itself structural factors are also at work. Just as the techniques of advocacy are themselves only adaptations to a particular form of proof, so the techniques of judicial reasoning are themselves significant only in a particular form of law. Law is made through the case law method both in the development of common law and the application of statutes. The rhetoric of justice in the form of general abstract rules is quite simply incompatible with the notion of case law. Levi notes that a general overall rule is useless in law because:

> It will have to operate at a level where it has no meaning. . . . The legal system does not work with the rule but at a much lower level. (Levi, 1949, p. 9)

A legal system based on case law (and even the states that boast codified law also use case law in a modified form) operates at the level of the concrete case: is highly particularistic. Hence the justification of excepting the specific case from the application of the general rule without destroying the general rule *per se*. The rhetoric and the law operate at two different levels, the abstract and the concrete, and the contradiction is operationally negated and a clear clash prevented by each being pigeon-holed out of the other's realm of discourse. The rhetoric is rarely actually denied, it is simply whittled away by exceptions, provisos, qualifications.

Law in this form is rather like a Russian doll. You begin with the rhetoric and a single, apparently definite, condition which on closer inspection turns out to contain another less clear condition which in turn opens up to reveal even more ifs and buts and vaguenesses, reducing so often to the unpredictability of 'it all depends on the circumstances'—what criteria we use in your case depends on your case. This form provides an extremely potent way of maintaining the facade of civil rights ideology—the first doll—while in fact allowing extensive *legal* police powers. Cases can readily accommodate both statements of general principle and the exceptions of particular circumstances. Thus an appeal on the grounds of abuse of a legal right can be rejected because of the circumstances of the particular case, while at the same time a grand statement reiterating that right is made. The conflicting rhetoric of due process and practical demands for crime control are thus both simultaneously maintained and the gap between rhetoric and practice is managed out of existence. Lawyers may boast of the flexibility and in-dividualised treatment afforded by case law but it also plays a potent role in maintaining the ideology of justice.[9]

This has implications for policy for it sets parameters on any possibility of lasting reform. Recommendations for changes in the law made by the Royal Commission on Criminal Procedure, the Fisher Report, committees on law reform, or whatever, must be seen as themselves subject to future change, future change which if the hypothesised development of case law noted in the previous section is anything to go by, all too often means a whittling away of the original principle. The spirit lingers in the rhetoric of justice but the qualifications and provisos of case law render it rather less effective. Lasting reform cannot be possible without some deeper change in the form of law itself.

But the nature of case law has implications not only for policy but for sociological understanding of the role of law in society, for the operation of dominant ideology and the democratic state. It has implications in particular for one area in which these three coalesce, in the idea of the rule of law.

## THE CASE LAW FORM AND THE RULE OF LAW

The principles of justice are part of the ideology of the democratic state not only in their substance but in a much more fundamental way, in the very idea that there should be principles at all, that those who wield the power of the state should not do so arbitrarily but should themselves be governed by law. The idea of legality itself is an essential ideological form of the democratic state; its rule is the rule of law.

The idea of the rule of law is central not just to the arena of criminal justice, perhaps the most explicitly coercive aspect of state–individual relations, but to sociological theories of law in general in capitalist society. One strand, epitomised by Weber (1954) and Neumann (1957) emphasises dependability or certainty as its one essential element; the rule of law is the rule of *known* law. Concerned more with civil than criminal law, they relate the development of law in capitalist society to the need for commerce to operate in a situation of certainty, in the knowledge that contracts could be relied on to be fulfilled or enforced. Second, E. P. Thompson has sparked off debate by challenging the crude Marxist notion that the rule of law is merely a mask for the rule of the dominant class. Though he qualified his argument as being only certainly applicable to eighteenth-century England, it has been generalised in debate to the question of the function of law in capitalist society in general.[10] He argues that the ideology of justice is no mere mask but also a potential for genuine transcendence of class interests: 'The law may be rhetoric but it need not be empty rhetoric'. (E. P. Thompson, 1975, p. 263).[11] There are two reasons for this. Class relations are expressed in law *'through the forms of law'* (*ibid.*, p. 262). These are independent of class interests and Thompson implies, a constraint upon them. What is more, people are not, says Thompson, mystified by the first man to put on a wig. The principles of justice, once declared, take on a force of their own in that they have to be lived up to if their ideological functions are to succeed. The rulers thus become 'prisoners of their own rhetoric' (*ibid.*, p. 263). The essential issue here is the *autonomy of law*, the idea of the rule of law above man as of theoretical as well as ideological validity.

For both these strands of theorising and debate on the rule of law the form of case law must raise serious questions, questions which have indeed been raised at various historical moments in the politics and ideology of Common Law.[12] Certainly one can find quotations from judges on the need for certainty in the law. In 1754 Lord Hardwicke noted: 'I think authorities established are so many laws and receding from them unsettles property; and uncertainty is the unavoidable consequence' (cited in Holdsworth, 1934, p. 188). But such statements jar so clearly not just with the practice of judges but with the *form* of the case law method, that one cannot help but speculate that Weber's description of a move to 'rational' law for the sake of certainty traces the development of an ideology of law rather than a description of either its practice or its form.

Case law is discretionary and particularistic; it does not operate at the level of general rules. What is more, as noted in Chapter 3, it only operates *post hoc*—it does not make law until *after* a dispute has made it into an issue. Of course there are precedents to constrain judgements. But they need only constrain the justification of the decision rather than the decision itself. Indeed the discretion invested in judges, and the fact that the case comes before them only after dispute, only because 'informed lawyers disagree' and can make out a case for both sides, means 'a judge's decision either way will not be considered a failure to perform his judicial responsibilities' (Greenawalt, cited in R. Cross, 1977, p. 221). What Hart (1961) calls the open texture of law allows wide scope in the use and application of precedent. Indeed precedents can be employed to do the exact opposite of their original use, as examples in this study show. The meaning attached to precedent deserves attention too. Holdsworth argues that the method of making law by precedent was only accepted historically by the judiciary on condition that it was *not* an overbearing constraint (Holdsworth, 1934, p. 180). This was accomplished by developing their own ideology of law. Coke, Hale, and Blackstone were all firm exponents of the view that decisions and precedents were *not law* but merely 'evidence of what the law is'. The result is that: 'The courts must decide what weight is to be attached to the evidence in different sets of circumstances'. Holdsworth concludes:

> The manner in which they have decided this question has left them many means of escape from the necessity of literal obedience to the general rule that decided cases must always be followed. (*ibid.*, p. 185)

Structurally indeed there *could not* historically have been a systematic following of precedents quite simply because there was no systematic reporting of cases until the end of the nineteenth century, a matter which provided further justification for the judges to ignore precedent on the basis that reports were not authoritative.[13] Cross suggests that with more systematic law reporting and restructuring of the courts, by the nineteenth century the idea of binding precedent had become more rigid (R. Cross, 1977, p. 23). But it did not last long, for he also observes that the English doctrine of precedent is *currently* in a state of flux (*ibid.*, p. 6). Though the Court of Appeal is still in theory bound by its own and the House of Lords' decisions, there are several well-known cases in which it has not followed them,[14] while in 1966 the House of Lords stated quite explicitly it need not be bound by its own precedents. This is not to say that precedent is never followed in the making of case law; it may even *usually* be followed. It is merely to say that it *need* not be a rigid constraint. Indeed the very degree of constraint involved is, it would seem, subject to the changing decisions of the judges themselves, the people it is supposed to constrain. The doctrine of precedent may thus be placed more aptly in the rhetoric rather than the actual procedure of justice. The doctrine of precedent may tell us where the ideology of the rule of law is grounded and how it is maintained, but it tells us very little about the practice of case law— not just because of judicial techniques to use and avoid precedent but because of the nature of the ideology of precedent and the *post hoc* discretionary particularistic form of the case law method.

The result is that the law is so far from being certain as to be almost impossible to pin down. This study would never have taken the shape it has if I had been able, as an observer in courts unread in law at all, to get a precise answer from the lawyers I eagerly asked what the law of search, or arrest, or the right to silence, actually was. The answer was a list of cases all with different specific lines—'in *R.* v. *Green* the decision was X but of course in *R.* v. *Brown* it was Y'— and so on. The textbooks offered the same, noting sometimes that the law on that point *may* be so and so. And soon it became clear that it was not my lack of legal learning that made the law so elusive: that was the nature of the law, a will-o'-the-wisp pausing but a moment before the next decision, and then only 'clear' for the particular circumstances of that particular case.

When law takes such a form, there *can be* no fixed or certain rule of law. The Weberian thesis of the bourgeois need for certain law must be challenged by even a perfunctory analysis of the form of law, especially in the common law systems of both the first capitalist society, Britain, and the most advanced, the United States, which illustrate the case law method *par excellence*. But it is not just common law that is based on cases; modern law *per se*, however codified in general, comes down in the end to application to concrete situations, to case law. Law in modern society,[15] far from being certain, is as elusive and as adaptable as a chameleon.

This elusiveness also plays its part in the mystique of law. What can be more mystical than a statement of what the law is which is not only veiled by the need to know where and how to look for it, but which turns out when you find it to be provisional, particular, and only really ascertainable for your specific question if you take it to court? The portrayal by Thompson—and others—of the mystique of law is too simple. People may not be bamboozled by the wigs and ceremony and jargon of the law, but they are quite likely to be bamboozled by the law itself. It is not just that they are in their ignorance puzzled by the law, it is also quite simply that the law *is* a puzzle. Its particularistic *post hoc* form inevitably makes it so.

But analysing the form of law undermines Thompson's argument in deeper ways. Thompson discusses the 'forms of law' by which he means procedures, but not the basic '*form*' of law, the nature of law itself. Nor does his analysis really distinguish between the general rhetoric and specific rules of law[16]. He equates them— 'the law may be rhetoric . . .'—but he is really talking only of the ideology of justice. On that level his point on the ideological availability of 'justice' to *all* of society is beyond reproach. Of course 'justice', 'equality', and 'liberty' have all been banners for all classes: it is the meaning they are invested with that ties them to one, and it is in the specific rulings of law that those meanings are defined and refined into the particular shape endorsed and enforceable by the state.

It is at that stage that Thompson would see class interests constrained by the need to abide by the rhetoric for ideological purposes, and by the 'forms of law', its logic, procedure, and rules. But the theory is too simple. It is not enough to say the rulers are 'prisoners of their own rhetoric', that the law cannot seem just 'without upholding its own logic and criteria of equity'. Studying the content of the law shows this is not necessarily what happens. The logic, rules, and procedures of the law, as this study has shown, far from being fixed constraints, are highly malleable. The question that must arise is rather: how is it possible for the ideological function to be fulfilled *without* overly constraining the rulers? What this study has tried to show in examining the management of the ideological gap between the rhetoric of justice and the content of law is precisely how judges can *both uphold*, even eulogise, the rhetoric yet simultaneously deny its applicability. The *'can'* is important, since they can also do quite the opposite, as the brief discussion in this study of the eighteenth-century judges, or the fuller one in Hay's of the eighteenth-century courts (Hay, 1975) shows. But the opportunity is always there, and it is there not just in the hypocrisy or reasoning powers of rulers but in the structure of legal procedures and the form of law. The 'forms of law' not only *express* constraints, they include methods for negating them.

This has a further implication. General theories of law too often analyse the role of law as though it were an ideological monolith. What this study underlines is the need to analyse the different aspects and levels of law with greater precision. If we separate out the rhetoric, substance, and—much deeper than Thompson's 'forms'—the basic form of law, we find not only that they are different elements but that the articulation of the different elements helps explain how the ideology *can* operate successfully *without* making the rulers of the state too extensively the prisoners of its rhetoric.

Returning to the debate between Thompson and a more directly economistic Marxism as to whether law is a mere mask for class interests or not, or indeed to any of the polarised conceptualisations of law posed in the sociological debates over law, one can perhaps conclude that the polarities lie not in the theoretical perspectives so much as in the law itself. The question may be less a matter of which of two alternative theories of the role of law in society is right, but of how it is possible for the law to present itself plausibly in such opposing ways, how it is possible for the contradictory theories to be posed in the first place. To examine the form of law in relation to the ideology of the rule of law is to gain some insights into *how* the law is able to contain—in both senses—internal contradictions. It may help us understand not only how the legal system can simultaneously maintain both due process and crime control, the prime concern of this study, but more broadly, how it can reproduce the ideology of justice while denying it, and *how* the state through law can give class-based ideas 'the form of universality' (Marx and Engels, 1965, p. 66).

There have been criticisms of the uncertainty of the case law method. Bentham likened it to making law for a dog—'You wait till he does it and then beat him.' The contemporary police lobby—just like that in 1912 seeking guidance over exactly what powers were available to the police in doing their job after two contradictory decisions in the courts—echo this, for it is in a sense seeking not so much *more* powers (they so often do have them *de facto* in case law) but *certain* powers. Academic lawyers still analyse specific areas of law and express anxiety over the gaps, loopholes, and uncertainties they find there. Ashworth (1979), for example, criticises loose phraseology in the law; he describes ambiguities in the operation of criminal justice, traces them to ambiguities in the conceptualisation of what criminal justice is for, and implies they must be made explicit, discussed, and resolved. For the policeman and the lawyer ambiguity in law is an anomaly to be cleared up. From a sociological perspective, however, such gaps and uncertainties are not contingent or anomalous but the inevitable product of the form of law—these are not weak points in the system but a source of *operational strength*—a crucial means by which the legal system is able to work at all—and of ideological strength—precisely what allows the law to be all things to all men, to contain contradictions, to manage the gap between what it does and what it should.

The rhetoric of law in capitalist society can thus safely extol the principles of legality or the rule of law, of a concept of justice geared to safeguarding the citizen from the state, of an impartial and universal classlessness in the idea of the equal legal subject. It can do so safely not only because the rhetoric of criminal justice is routinely subverted in practice by its practitioners, whether through the non-legal motivation of the policeman on the beat or through the reasoning powers of the High Court judges. Nor indeed only because the rhetoric of equality is negated by the economic structure, by the disconsonance between legal ideology and social reality epitomised in Anatole France's much-quoted observation that the law equally forbids rich and poor to sleep under bridges and beg, by the fact that the law *cannot* allocate equal rights in an unequal society (Marx, 1875, p.16; Corrigan and Sayer, 1979, p. 12).

The disconsonance can also exist *and be resolved* within the law itself; the ideology can·also be managed out of existence within the law's own institutional structure.[17] It is certainly true that the law or any other ideology must not be dismissed as merely empty rhetoric; it must be taken seriously as a set of ideas with its own complex structure, substance, and methods. The operation of dominant ideology must be studied not only in terms of how it is put into practice in social interaction, not only in terms of its interrelationship with the social and economic structure of society, but also in terms of its own internal form and dynamics.

# Notes

CHAPTER 1

1 Some of the problems on which this book is based were first raised in two
  exploratory articles which this chapter draws on and develops: McBarnet,
  1976, 1978(a).
2 The term 'judge' is used loosely here to cover any judge of the facts other than
  the jury, e.g. magistrate, or sheriff.
3 HMSO Cmnd 7670, 7676. For Scotland see the summary at paragraph 7.19.
  For England see Table 4.8.
4 See, for example, on 'prejudices' and variations Bottomley, 1973; Hood, 1962,
  1972. On the police see Cain, 1971, 1973; Skolnick, 1966; Piliavin and Briar,
  1964; Young, 1971. On lawyers see Newman, 1966; Blumberg, 1967; Skolnick,
  1967; Baldwin and McConville, 1977. On courts see Carlen, 1976; Garfinkel,
  1956; Bottoms and McClean, 1976; Hetzler and Kanter, 1974.
5 A study of the jury.


CHAPTER 2

1 Analysed in succeeding chapters.


CHAPTER 3

1 *The Times*, 15 June, 1978; *Guardian*, 8 January 1979.
2 The Director of Public Prosecutions: *Guardian*, 8 January 1979.
3 This and the following section are based on and developed from a previous
  article, McBarnet, 1978(a).
4 See, for example, Dell, 1971; Baldwin and McConville, 1977.
5 In Scotland there is a duty solicitor scheme which was extended for the first
  time to the district courts (the nearest equivalent in what is rather a different
  court structure) in 1975.
6 See Chapter 4.
7 See Chapter 2 and Chapter 6 for further details on corroboration.
8 Sir David McNee, Metropolitan Police Commissioner, *The Times*, 15 June
  1978.
9 See Chapter 2.
10 See this chapter, on 'The Right to Silence?'
11 A random sample from a Glasgow court's files.
12 Baldwin and McConville, 1977; and see Chapter 4.
13 See Cox, 1975.

14 For example, Mungham and Thomas, 1976.
15 In England. Full details are being written up by the author in a separate study of the jury.
16 See Chapter 8 for a discussion of the implications of the *post hoc* nature of case law.

1 Chapters 4 and 5 draw on and develop a section of 'Pre-trial Procedures and the Construction of Conviction' (McBarnet, 1976).
2 Baldwin and McConville, 1977.
3 As in for example, Chapter 3, p. 59.
4 In Scots law a distinction is drawn between a necessary attack in the course of making a defence case and a general attack on character (Renton and Brown, 1972, p. 365).
5 This example, demonstrating a point of English law, is taken from observations in English courts, in the course of a separate study by the author of the jury system.

1 In some cases the burden is shifted by statute or presumption. See Chapter 6.
2 Discussed in Chapter 6.

1 Whether this is an entirely accurate version of the Commissioner's evidence is less significant than the fact that this was the ideology made available to the public.
2 Indeed the Committee recommended a marked extension of this. If the judge or jury should have doubts about Crown evidence, the accused's silence should effectively be used to wipe them out (Thomson, 1975, p. 190).
3 Remember Sir Robert Mark's comment Chapter 5, p. 81
4 *Knowles* v. *H.M.Adv*, unreported.
5 *R* v. *Gilbert*, 1977.
6 *Maitland* v. *Glasgow Corporation*, 1947.
7 Discussed in detail in a separate study of the jury (McBarnet).
8 Chapter 3, p. 57
9 Frazier, 1979.
10 For example: Davies, 1971.
11 See Hepworth and Turner, 1979.
12 Though 'neutral acts' require proof of *mens rea*.
13 In Scotland two co-accomplices will do.
14 See Chapter 5, p. 92
15 On the jury (McBarnet).

16 It would have been interesting to note not just the percentage of *cases* dealt with without a jury, but the percentage of *trials*. This information is not, however, available in the Criminal Statistics or from the Home Office.

CHAPTER 7

1 In England this refers to the magistrates' courts. In Scotland 'non-jury' trials and guilty pleas are dealt with not just by lay magistrates (indeed lay magistrates operate only on the fringes of criminal justice) and stipendiary magistrates but also by sheriffs sitting without a jury who deal with half of non-indictment prosecutions (Walker, 1976, p. 238). In England, though not in Scotland, the defendant can choose whether to be tried by jury or by magistrates for a range of offences, though there are systematic pressures towards 'opting' for summary justice just as there are towards 'opting' for a guilty plea. For a start there is a much lower maximum penalty, six months' imprisonment or £1000 fine (raised from three months and £500 by the Criminal Law Act 1977); second the defendant cannot be committed to the Crown Court for sentence. These are described by Smith and Hogan (1977) as 'bonuses', though of course one could as readily interpret them as inducements.

2 That is, for law and justice. They *do* fill other ideological roles, e.g. on the virtues of employment and family life.

3 Extended to the lower courts only in the 1975 reorganisation, or at least renaming, of the district courts.

4 The report retains discretion in the award of legal aid in cases triable only by magistrates, changing the emphasis from the need to find grounds to award it to the need to find grounds to deny it, but employing the same basic criteria.

5 James Report, 1975, Appendix.

6 See Chapter 2.

7 See Rouse Jones, 1953, p. 6.

8 See Thompson, 1950.

9 Arguile, 1969; Lords Debate on the Magistrates' Courts, Hansard, 1952; Walker, 1976.

10 The *Weekly News*.

11 See Brogden, 1979.

12 See this Chapter, p. 137

13 Less so in Scotland; see note 1.

14 See Chapter 3, p. 33.

CHAPTER 8

1 Taylor *et al.* (1971); Young (1971); Cohen (1971).

2 The inevitable exceptions are: in England, the prosecutor's right of appeal from a magistrates' court where the magistrate has dismissed a case on a point of law; in Scotland the prosecutor may not appeal against the decision of a High Court or Sheriff Court with a jury but may appeal by stated case against a summary acquittal. In addition, Andrew Ashworth has kindly pointed out that the Criminal Justice Act 1972 s. 36 introduced an opportunity to clear up disputed

points of law even if the accused was acquitted, though he also notes that this is statistically insignificant.

3 Developed from a discussion in McBarnet 1978(b).

4 Surveys may not suggest any overwhelming belief by the British public at large in the impartiality of justice, but there is sufficient indignation expressed by middle-class liberal camps, when crime control or *raison d'état* too explicitly steamrolls over civil liberties, to suggest a belief on their part at least that the law is, or should normally be, geared to civil rights. Witness not just the liberal reaction to the law and order campaign of the 1970s but to specific incidents like the Hosenball affair (in 1977) or jury vetting in 1979.

5 See Chapter 3, p. 46.

6 See Chapter 3, p. 47.

7 See Chapter 3, p. 63.

8 See Chapter 3, p. 62.

9 See McBarnet, 1978(b); Kinsey, 1978; Picciotto, 1979.

10 See National Deviancy Conference/Conference of Socialist Economists proceedings, 1979.

11 This echoes Carson, 1974.

12 For example see Horwitz, 1977, Chapter 1 on early nineteenth-century American criticisms of the unpredictability of Common Law, or Bentham (discussed later).

13 T. Ellis-Lewis, 1930–32; Holdsworth, 1934.

14 R. Cross, 1977, pp. 105, 118.

15 At least on the basis of this analysis of *criminal* law.

16 Despite separating them before he actually engages in discussing them (1975, p. 260).

17 This is not of course to deny in any way that the structure and form of the law need themselves to be explained and related (though on the basis of two-way interaction rather than economic determinism) to their material base. (See for example Pashukanis, 1978.) It is merely to pose a supplementary issue.

# References

Alderson, J. C. and P. J. Stead, *The Police We Deserve* (Wolfe, 1973).

Archbold, *Pleading, Evidence and Practice in Criminal Cases*, 40th edn (Sweet & Maxwell, 1979).

Arguile, R., *Criminal Procedure* (Butterworths, 1969).

Armstrong, G. and M. Wilson, 'City Politics and Deviance Amplification', in L. Taylor and I. Taylor (eds.), *Politics and Deviance* (Penguin, 1973).

Ashworth, J. A., 'A threadbare principle', *Criminal Law Review*, (July 1978).

—— 'Concepts of criminal justice', *Criminal Law Review*, (July 1979).

Atkinson, J. M. and P. Drew, *Order in Court* (Macmillan, 1979).

Baldwin, J. and M. McConville, *Negotiated Justice*, (Martin Robertson, 1977).

Blumberg, A. S., *Criminal Justice* (Quadrangle, 1967).

Bottomley, A. K., *Decisions in the Penal Process* (Martin Robertson, 1973).

Bottoms, A. E. and J. D. McClean, *Defendants in the Criminal Process* (Routledge & Kegan Paul, 1976).

Boulton, W., *Conduct and Etiquette at the Bar* (Butterworth, 1975).

Box, S. and K. Russell, 'The politics of discreditability: disarming complaints against the police', *Sociological Review* (May 1975).

Brogden, M. 'All police is cunning bastards'. Paper presented at the BSA Conference on Law and Society (1979).

Cain, M., 'On the beat', in S. Cohen (ed.), *Images of Deviance* (Penguin, 1971).

—— *Society and The Policeman's Role* (Routledge & Kegan Paul, 1973).

Carlen, P., *Magistrates' Justice* (Martin Robertson, 1976).

Carson, W. G., '*Symbolic and instrumental dimensions of early factory legislation*', in R. Hood (ed.), *Crime, Criminology and Public Policy* (Heinemann, 1973).

—— 'The sociology of crime and the emergence of criminal laws', in P. Rock and M. McIntosh (eds.), *Deviance and Social Control* (Tavistock, 1974).

Cockburn, A. W., '*In Lumine,* an Address on Advocacy' (Faculty of Law, University of Southampton, 1952).

Coddington, F. J., *Advice on Advocacy in the Lower Courts* (Justice of the Peace Ltd, 1954).

Cohen, S., 'Mods Rockers and the rest' in W. G. Carson and P. Wiles (eds.), *Sociology of Crime and Delinquency* (Martin Robertson, 1971).

Corrigan, P. and D. Sayer, 'How the law rules'. Paper presented at the BSA Conference on Law and Society (1979).

Coull, J. W. and E. W. Merry, *Principles and Practice of Scots Law* (Butterworth, 1971).

Cox, B., *Civil Liberties in Britain* (Penguin, 1975).

Criminal Law Revision Committee, *11th Report*: Evidence (HMSO Cmnd 4991, 1972).

Criminal Statistics, England and Wales, 1978. (HMSO, Cmnd 7670, 1979).

Criminal Statistics, Scotland 1978. (HMSO, Cmnd 7676, 1979).

Cross, Lord, 'The lawyer and justice', Presidential address to The Holdsworth Club (University of Birmingham, 1973).

Cross, R., *On Evidence* (Butterworths, 1974).

—— *Precedent in English Law*, 3rd edn. (Oxford University Press, 1977).

Darbyshire, P., '*The role of the justices' clerk and the court clerk*', Ph.D. Thesis, Faculty of Law, Birmingham University (1978).

Davies, C., 'Pre-trial imprisonment, *British Journal of Criminology* (1971).

Dell, S., *Silence In Court*. Occasional Papers on Social Administration, 42 (Bell, 1971).

Devlin, J. D., *Criminal Courts and Procedure* (Butterworths 1960).

Ellis-Lewis, T., 'The history of judicial precedent', *Law Quarterly Review*, (1930–32).

Fisher, H., Report of an inquiry into the Confait case (HMSO, 1977).

Frazier, C. E., 'Appearance, demeanour and backstage negotiations', *International Journal of the Sociology of Law*, Vol.7, No. 2 (May 1979).

Friedman, L., 'A historical study of criminal justice'. Paper presented at the Centre for Socio-Legal Studies, Oxford (1978).

Garfinkel, H., 'Conditions of successful degradation ceremonies', *American Journal of Sociology*, 61, (1956).

Gordon, G. H., 'The burden of proof on the accused', *Scots Law Times News* (1968).

Hall, S., C. Chritcher, T. Jefferson, J. Clarke and B. Roberts, *Policing the Crisis; Mugging the State and Law and Order* (Macmillan, 1978).

Halsbury, H. S., *Statutes of England*, 3rd edn (Butterworths, 1969).

Hart, H. L. A., *The Concept of Law* (Clarendon Press, 1961).

Hay, D., 'Property, authority and the law', in Hay *et al.* (eds.), *Albion's Fatal Tree* (Allen Lane, 1975).

Hepworth, M. and B. Turner, 'Confessions: guilt and responsibility'. Paper presented at the BSA Conference on Law and Society (1979).

Hetzler, A. N. and C. H. Kanter, 'Informality and the court', in S. F. Sylvester and E. Sagarin (eds.), *Politics and Crime* (Praeger, 1974).

Heydon, J. D., *Cases and Materials on Evidence* (Stevens, 1975).

Hilbery, M., *Duty and Art in Advocacy* (Stevens, 1975).

Holdsworth, W., 'Case Law', *Law Quarterly Review*, Vol. 50, 180. (1934).

Home Office Circular No. 31 (1964).

Hood, R. G., *Sentencing in Magistrates' Courts* (Stevens, 1962).

—— *Sentencing the Motoring Offender* (Heinemann, 1972).

Horwitz, M. J., *The Transformation of American Laws 1760–1860* (Harvard, 1977).

Inbau, F. E. and J. R. Reid, *Criminal Interrogations and Confessions*, 2nd edn. (Williams & Wilkins Co., 1974).

Inman, M., Paper presented at the Conference on Law and Psychology, Oxford (1978).

James Report, Cmnd. 6323 (Home Office, Lord Chancellor's Office, 1975).

King, M., *Bail or Custody?* (Cobden Trust, 1971).

Kinsey, R., 'Marxism and the law: preliminary analyses', *British Journal of Law and Society*, Vol. 5, No. 2 (Winter 1978).

Lafave, W. R. and Remington, 'Controlling the police: the judge's role in making and reviewing law enforcement decisions', *Michigan Law Review*, 63 (1975).

Langbein, J. H., *Torture and the Law of Proof* (University of Chicago Press, 1977).

Leigh, L. H., *Police Powers in England and Wales* (Butterworths, 1975).

Levi, E. H., *An Introduction to Legal reasoning* (University of Chicago Press, 1949).

McBarnet, D. J., 'Pre-trial procedures and the construction of conviction', in P. Carlen (ed.), *Sociological Review Monograph on the Sociology of Law* (Keele University, 1976).

—— 'The police and the state: arrest, legality and the law', in G. Littlejohn *et al.* (eds.), *Power and the State* (Croom Helm, 1978a).

—— 'The Fisher Report on the Confait case: four issues', *Modern Law Review* (May 1978b).

McIntosh, M., 'Changes in the organisation of thieving', in S. Cohen (ed.), *Images of Deviance* (Penguin, 1971).

Mack, J. A., 'Full-time miscreants', *Modern Law Review* (May 1976).

Marx, K., *Critique of the Gotha Programme* (1875) in K. Marx and F. Engels, *Selected Works* (Lawrence & Wishart, 1968).

Mungham, G. and P. Thomas, 'Advocacy and the Solicitor-Advocate in magistrates' courts in England and Wales', *International Journal of the Sociology of Law* (May 1979).

—— *A Report on the Duty Solicitor Scheme Operating in Cardiff Magistrates' Courts 1973–74* (University College, Cardiff, 1976).

Napley, D., *The Technique of Persuasion*, 2nd edn. (Sweet & Maxwell, 1975).

National Deviancy Conference/Conference of Socialist Economists, *Capitalism and the Rule of Law* (Hutchinson, 1979).

Neumann, F., *The Democratic and Authoritarian state* (Collier Macmillan, 1957).

Newman, D. J., *Conviction* (Little, Brown, 1966).

Packer, H. L., 'Two models of criminal justice', *University of Pennsylvania Law review*, 113 (1964).

Pashukanis, E. B., *Law and Marxism: a general theory* (Ink Links, 1978).

Picciotto, S., 'The Theory of the state, class struggle and the rule of law', in NDC/CSE, *Capitalism and the Rule of Law* (Hutchinson, 1979).

Piliavin, I. and S. Briar, 'Police encounters with juveniles', *American Journal of Sociology*, 70 (1964).

Price, J. P., *The English Legal System* (M and E Handbooks, 1979).

Release Lawyers Group, *Guilty until Proved Innocent?* (Release, 1973).

Renton, R. W. and H. H. Brown, *Criminal Procedure According to the Law of Scotland*, 4th edn. (Green, 1972).

Rouse Jones, L., *Magistrates' Courts* (Sweet & Maxwell, 1953).

Royal Commission on Legal Services, Report (HMSO, Cmnd. 7648, 1979).

Skolnick, J., *Justice without Trial* (Wiley, 1966).

—— 'Law and conflict resolution', *Journal of Conflict Resolution*, XI (1967).

Smith, J. C. and B. Hogan, *Criminal Law*, 4th edn. (Butterworths, 1977).

Sykes, R. and J. Clark, 'A theory of deference exchange in police–civilian encounters', *American Journal of Sociology*, 81, 3 (1975).

Taylor, I., 'Soccer consciousness and Soccer hooliganism', in S. Cohen (ed.), *Images of Deviance* (Penguin, 1971).

Taylor, I., P. Walton, and J. Young, *Critical Criminology* (Routledge & Kegan Paul, 1975).

Thomas, P., 'Plea bargaining in England', *Journal of Criminal Law and Criminology*, Vol. 69, No. 2 (1978).

Thompson, F., *Magna Carta* (University of Minnesota Press, 1950).

Thompson, E. P., *Whigs and Hunters* (Allen Lane, 1975).

Thomson Committee, *Criminal Procedure in Scotland* (Second Report, HMSO, Cmnd. 6218, 1975).

Walker, A. G. and N. M. Walker, *The Law of Evidence in Scotland* (Wm. Hodge and Co. Ltd, 1975).

Walker, A. G., *The Scottish Legal System* (Green, 1969).

Weber, M., *On Law and Economy in Society*, ed. by M. Rheinstein, (Harvard University Press, 1954).

Widgery, Report of the Departmental Committee on Legal Aid in Criminal Court Proceedings (Home Office, Cmnd. 2934, 1966).

Young, J., *The Drugtakers* (Paladin, 1971).

Zander, M., 'Unrepresented defendants in the criminal courts', *Criminal Law Review* (1969).

—— 'Access to a solicitor in the police station', *Criminal Law Review* (1972).

# Index of Cases

Numbers in bold type refer to pages in this book where the cases are mentioned.

# Index of Statutes

# Author Index